Market Timing for the Nineties

THE FIVE KEY SIGNALS FOR
WHEN TO BUY, HOLD, AND SELL

Market Timing for the Nineties

THE FIVE KEY SIGNALS FOR WHEN TO BUY, HOLD, AND SELL

Revised and Updated

Stephen Leeb

with Roger S. Conrad

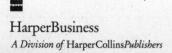

HarperBusiness
A Division of HarperCollinsPublishers

This book is dedicated to my loving and always supportive family, Donna, Timmy, and Will.

—STEPHEN LEEB

To my parents and my wife, Sarah, for all their love and support.

—ROGER S. CONRAD

A hardcover edition of this book was published in 1993 by HarperBusiness, a division of HarperCollins Publishers.

HarperCollins books may be purchased for educational, business, or sales promotional use. For information please write: Special Markets Department, HarperCollins Publishers, Inc., 10 East 53rd Street, New York, NY 10022.

First paperback edition published 1994.

Designed by Irving Perkins Associates

The Library of Congress has catalogued the hardcover edition as follows:

Leeb, Stephen, 1946–
    Market timing for the nineties : the five key signals for when to
buy, hold, and sell / Stephen Leeb with Roger S. Conrad. — 1st ed.
        p.   cm.
    Includes index.
    ISBN 0-88730-641-1
    1. Investment analysis.   2. Stocks.   3. Economic forecasting.
I. Conrad, Roger S.   II. Title.   III. Title: Market timing for the
90's.
HG4529.L443   1993
332.63'22—dc20   92-54733

ISBN 0-88730-689-6 (pbk.)
94 95 96 97 98 PS/RRD 10 9 8 7 6 5 4 3 2 1

Contents

Preface

I WROTE THIS BOOK to share with you the approach that has made me one of America's top market timers for the past five years, and a top stock picker as well.

Mastering the market is not as impossible as you might think. The data that make stocks tick are accessible and easy to understand. You just have to know where to look and be willing to use a bit of common sense.

I've been in the investment advisory business for more than sixteen years. When I started, I can admit now, I didn't know a whole lot about the stock market. But I had one thing going for me—strong analytical skills, gained in my years in academia. In other words, I knew how to look at a complex situation, such as the stock market, objectively, gather in masses of data, and draw conclusions. I did this over and over and over.

For example, the conventional wisdom had it—still has it—that rapid profit growth means higher stock prices. I decided to test this and found that the opposite was true: Most often, when profits begin to soar a bull market is on its last legs.

As I continued, I began to put together a cohesive view of what drives the stock market, and I was shocked to discover that this is something most other analysts utterly lack.

If you look at most other investment books, you'll find that the authors offer "systems" for investing. They may advise buying only stocks with low price-to-earnings ratios (P/Es), for example, or selling whenever a stock has dropped by a certain percentage.

There is nothing necessarily wrong with such rules. But they are incomplete; they say nothing about the big picture. It's as if someone from Mars came down to Earth and was handed a baby and given rules about how to change the baby's diaper and feed it with a bottle, but with no one remembering to mention the fact that the baby was going to grow up into a child and then an adult.

If you understand what really drives the market, then you can deal in a rational way with stocks' daily gyrations. If you have a guiding sense of the big picture, you will be in a position to buy when the market is starting a long-term uptrend and to get out when stocks are embarking upon a long-term downtrend. You'll keep your head in crises and be able to ignore most of the nonsense that you will hear on the airways and read in the financial press.

So what drives the market? The economy and, in particular, prospects for sustainable economic growth. Over the long run, economic trends always determine what the market will do.

Other factors may intervene temporarily, such as the crisis in the Persian Gulf did in late 1990. But always the market will revert back to the path dictated by the outlook for sustainable growth. What makes this book different from, and far more valuable than, the typical investment guide? It explains, as simply as possible, the interrelationships between the market and the economy, and tells you how to apply them for long-term investment success.

I can hear your question now: How can I possibly forecast the economy when trained economists so often fail? The answer is that forecasting the economy's effect on stocks, bonds, gold or any other market doesn't mean predicting next quarter's gross national product or next month's unemployment report. It all really boils down to that one simple principle: Stocks live and die on prospects for sustainable economic growth.

If the current level of growth is sustainable—or likely to increase—stocks have a lot of room to run. But if growth is steaming ahead, chances are the market is about to run out of gas. History has proven time and again this simple relationship: Bull markets run on empty, but die on full.

What determines whether or not growth is sustainable? To a large degree, it's inflation. Inflation must remain under control for a bull market in stocks to thrive. Other factors may cause stocks to dip from time to time. But in the end, lower inflation means sustainable growth and a rising stock market. Rising inflation means a bear market in stocks is near.

I've combed through about a century's worth of statistics on the market and the economy to find the most reliable forecasters of this relationship between inflation, growth, and stocks—literally millions of statistics on market indexes, unemployment, bond yields, and so on. You name it, I've looked at it.

For the past sixteen years, I've put these relationships to the ultimate test: I have used them in managing my clients' money and in writing my financial newsletters. I don't think I'm boasting when I say my results have been excellent.

The primary goal of this book—what makes it different from any other investment guide I've seen—is to teach you how to forecast the market the way I do, by looking at the only thing that matters: the relationship between the market and the economy.

A secondary goal is to show how a few common-sense rules can make you a better stock picker than virtually any mutual fund manager around. Whether you're an individual investor or an institutional money manager, I firmly believe this is the only investment book you'll ever need to buy.

Yes, this stuff really does work. And to apply it you need access to a public library, a five-dollar calculator, and of course this book. That kind of investment in time and money will indeed put you many steps ahead of almost all the professionals in this business.

Stephen Leeb

Acknowledgments

Roger and I are deeply grateful to all those who helped us bring this book from idea to print. First, thanks go to our agent Al Zuckerman, who made us realize that it is possible to write a technical book in readable form. Special kudos also to our editor Cynthia Barrett at HarperCollins, who helped us achieve that lofty goal.

To Walter Pearce, Allie Ash, and Brian Smith, we offer our gratitude for their support and encouragement throughout the life of this project. Thanks also to the staff of Personal Finance, especially design editor George Howell, who provided invaluable help in preparing the many charts and graphs.

Finally, we'd like to thank our colleague Soula Stefanopoulos and my wife, Donna Leeb. Their careful reading and editing at each stage helped keep the project in focus and was essential to ensuring accuracy and consistency.

1

Inflation:
The Key to the Market

"TAKE THE MONEY AND RUN." That's what I told friends when they were offered $600,000 for their home in Connecticut. But they ignored me.

My friend Richard and his wife, Ellen, had bought the place five years earlier for "only" $250,000. Now their agent was telling them to hold out for at least $625,000. And they believed him instead of me.

After all, it was August 1987, the heyday of the roaring Reagan era. Stocks had been stampeding upward for years, and real estate prices were sky-high. It was no time to think small, or so my friends and many others like them thought.

Events proved them right, at first. Three more potential buyers cropped up, and within a few weeks Richard and Ellen had accepted an offer for $615,000.

Still, my pals were in no hurry to settle. They dithered over paying for a $1,000 fence around the swimming pool. And they put off the closing so they could spend one last Thanksgiving in the country.

As it turned out, they didn't have much to be thankful for. October 19, 1987, dawned with the Dow Jones Industrial Average at 2300. By the end of the day, this stock index had plunged over five hundred points, the biggest one-day drop in history. That very evening, the buyers withdrew their offer.

Richard and Ellen's house went unsold for three years, when they unloaded it for only half of what they initially wanted. And they were among the fortunate. Thousands of people lost their livelihoods due to the crash of 1987.

STALLING ON FULL

How did I know in August 1987 that the go-go days were drawing to a close? Because I realized that the great bull market in stocks was about to end. It was stocks' meteoric rise, more than anything else, that was pushing up real estate prices. Once the bubble burst, I reasoned, everything would come crashing down.

The economic boom that had begun back in 1982 had caused the stock prices of even the stodgiest companies to triple in just five years. And just about everyone thought this boom would go on forever.

It was tough not to get caught up in the euphoria of the times; most of my friends did. But I make my living by following indicators, raw numbers that represent time-tested relationships. And everything I saw at that time told me the stock market's bullish days were numbered no matter what the gurus of the day were saying.

It wasn't that I actually saw something that virtually no one else did. I didn't have any "secret" indicators or a crystal ball.

The signs of impending doom were available to anyone who bothered to pick up a morning paper or clicked on the evening news during the summer of 1987. In fact, the public was truly bombarded with all of the tell-tale signs that a market top was close at hand.

The problem was that practically everyone on Wall Street, as well as Main Street U.S.A., mistook what I saw as clear-cut warning signs of a coming crash for confirmation that the bull market in stocks had a long way to go.

The reason for their mistake may seem confusing at first. But it's very understandable. In fact, it explains why most people are invariably caught in the market at tops and are left out of the fabulous buying opportunities at market bottoms.

Ironically, the biggest sign that stocks were about to go dixie in August 1987 was the economy's robust health. Think about that. The single biggest tipoff that stocks were headed south was that the economy was growing far too quickly.

Most investors believe that a growing economy is good for stocks; that included my friends Richard and Ellen. The truth is, it's the *potential* for faster growth that fuels bull markets. The faster the economy grows, the less likely its rate of growth can be sustained over the long pull. And once it inevitably starts to slow, stocks always tank.

In August 1987, the economy was running at a terrific clip. Unemployment was dropping quickly. In fact, anyone who picked up *The New York Times* want ads could see that they were thick with unfilled jobs. Industrial production was rising to levels not seen since the 1960s. Consumers were spending more and everyone was borrowing to buy even more.

It was also the age of the "can't lose" investment. According to the "experts," it didn't matter how much you borrowed. Stocks were soaring to new all-time highs. And leveraged buyouts—à la Michael Milken—were the rage.

All of these signs of strong economic performance were seen by investors as favorable to stocks. But I knew from my studies of market history that precisely the opposite was true: these were terrible signs for stocks. The bull's days were numbered.

You see, all of these tell-tale signs weren't signaling that even greater prosperity lay ahead. They were tipoffs that growth was peaking. Inflation—the ultimate enemy of stocks—was on the warpath.

Inflation is essentially the rate at which prices for goods and services are increasing throughout the economy. It's the trend in inflation that ultimately determines whether or not economic growth is sustainable. Rising inflation is invariably a sign that growth is not sustainable. Falling inflation signals that it is.

The economy's rapidly rising inflation rate by mid-1987 was the key to anticipating the stock market's inevitable demise that year. While Wall Street was cheerleading the economy on, rapidly rising employment was triggering a shortage of workers and a boost in wages. Spurts in industrial production were sending commodity prices soaring. Interest rates were starting to tick up. Prices were climbing across the board.

In short, stocks' eternal nemesis—rising inflation—was staging a comeback. That, more than anything else, was my sure and clear sign that the rate of economic growth in mid-1987 was simply not sustainable. Stocks were headed for a fall and so, not surprisingly, was New York area real estate.

HOW FAST IS TOO FAST?

Ultimately, stock prices reflect one thing: What investors think of companies' future earnings. When the economy is expected to grow, corporate profits are too, so most stock prices rise. The reverse also holds: When the economy is expected to move slowly or not at all, stock prices fall.

Note that stock-price moves are based on expectations of economic growth, not on what's going on now or what happened last week. It didn't matter a hoot, for example, that economic data were as rosy as could be in October 1987. The crash anticipated the negative effects of rising inflation.

As I'll explain below, economic growth is stymied first and foremost by inflation. So whenever inflation flares up, the smart money invested in stocks heads for the exits. It knows that sometime soon, projections for economic growth will drop and stocks right along with them. Only when inflation is moderate, or falling, do wise investors reenter the stock market in full force.

Because inflation is the tell-tale sign of an overheating economy, it affects each of the other core indicators I discuss in this book: commodity prices, unemployment, interest rates, money supply, and stocks' price-to-earnings ratios.

In fact, as we'll see in later chapters, these indicators are best understood in light of inflation. A large part of their success is based on how well they reflect the trend in inflation.

PUBLIC ENEMY NUMBER ONE

Because of inflation's ability to choke off economic growth, it is stocks' public enemy number one. Don't get me wrong. In and of itself, inflation is not bad for stocks or the economy. Since World War II, in fact, the U.S. economy has always had some inflation, and stocks have kept rising nonetheless.

From 1947 to 1965, for example, inflation, as measured by the consumer price index (CPI), averaged 1.7 percent annually, while stocks rose at a 10.5 percent annual rate. Including dividends, stocks' annual return for those eighteen years averaged a sparking 15.7 percent.

It's only when inflation is rising steeply that growth—and the stock market—are at risk. By the summer of 1987, for example, the Producer Price Index (PPI) was climbing at about a 4.5 percent annual rate. Moreover, that was about eight points greater than the 4 percent rate at which the PPI was falling a year earlier.

Even more ominous, commodity prices were soaring at a better than 30 percent rate. In other words, inflation was high and rising. That was a sure-fire sign that the current rate of economic growth could not be sustained. And it sounded the death knell for the great bull market, which had begun back in 1982.

Think of the economy as a train. The Federal Reserve, this country's central bank, is the train's chief engineer. Like a train, the economy has a top speed at which it can run without overheating.

At that speed, the economy is humming along beautifully. Below that speed, it can grow even faster. In both scenarios, stocks prosper because corporate earnings are likely to keep rising.

Past the top speed, however, things get ugly. The engine "overheats." In economic terms that translates into inflation—rising prices as demand outstrips supply.

History is full of examples of inflation raging out of control and destroying economies: Germany after World War I and Latin America in the 1980s are two prime examples. In both cases, price increases raged out of control. Money lost all value, paralyzing the will for businesses to invest, sending economic growth to a screeching halt.

In the later stages, domestic and foreign investors pulled their money out of local banks and into foreign ones, further drying up capital sources. Grocery store prices rose hourly.

Local stock markets in such situations can become virtually worthless. In such hyperinflationary conditions, economic trains inevitably jump off the track, and crash and burn.

Fortunately, since World War II, America has been spared the ravages of hyperinflation. The reason: When our economic train "overheats," the Fed typically "hits the brakes" to slow it down, long before a crisis erupts. It does this by raising interest rates, the subject of Chapter 4.

In early 1980, for example, the Fed jacked up short-term interest rates to post–Civil War highs. Within weeks the economic train stopped moving—a major recession hit. Inflation quickly fell from an annual rate of about 15 percent to 10 percent.

The Fed's careful watch over our economic train severely limits hyperinflation's threat to the economy and stocks. But when the central bank does hit the brakes, the results for stocks are often equally disastrous.

Just like on a braking train, the consequences of economic braking are not pretty: recession. Thousands of people are knocked out of their jobs. Businesses fail. And rapidly falling economic growth means lower stock prices.

And the higher the inflation before the brakes are hit, the worse the carnage. The Fed's anti-inflation moves in 1929 and 1987, for example, triggered the two greatest sell-offs for stocks in this century.

In other words, when inflation raises its ugly head, stocks are in trouble regardless of what the Federal Reserve does. If the Fed lets inflation rage out of control, it runs the risk of hyperinflation and sending the stock market to virtually worthless levels. But if the Fed fights inflation by slamming on the economic train's brakes (raising interest rates), economic growth will suffer and stocks will slide into the abyss.

RUNNING COOL

The good news is that in the middle of a recession, the economic train is just starting to leave the station and its engine is cool. This means that the economy can grow much faster, without igniting inflation.

For the first few hundred yards, the train's speed can increase from one to fifty miles an hour—a fifty-to-one gain—without reaching maximum speed. In other words, the annual rate of economic growth can rise from, say, 1 to 4 percent—a fourfold increase—without igniting inflation.

Stocks respond to that potential for growth by rising sharply, often long before the economy has actually shown real signs of growth.

Consider the recession of 1990–91. From their lows in January 1991 to their highs in April of the same year, stocks rose over 20 percent. But the economy showed signs of recovery much later, in May and June.

INFLATION AND STOCKS

The relationship I've described in the above train analogy has held true time and time again. In fact, it's no exaggeration to say that the history of the stock market is essentially a history of inflation.

One of the most important lessons I've learned is this: The bigger the rise in inflation, the more likely that economic growth will tank, taking stock prices with it. The lower the rate of inflation, the more likely stocks are to rise.

The chart on the following page shows this relationship clearly. I've divided the last seventy years into nine periods, each according to the rate of inflation as measured by the Consumer Price Index, or CPI. (The CPI is a weighted average of retail prices for a basket of goods and services bought by the "average" American.) Then, I classified each of these nine periods into four major categories:

- *Deflation:* On average, the CPI dropped 6.4 percent annually. This includes 1929–32.
- *Stable prices:* On average, the CPI dropped 0.2 percent annually. This includes 1921–29 and 1934–40.
- *Declining* or *moderate inflation:* On average, the CPI has increased 2.5 percent annually.
- *Rapid inflation:* On average, the CPI has risen 7 percent annually. This was the case from 1965 to 1981, a phenomenally bad time for stocks.

THE IMPACT OF INFLATION
(Annual Changes)

		Inflation*	Stocks	Bonds	Precious Metals
Deflation:	1929–32	−6.4%	−21.2%	5.0%	−19.8%
Stable	1921–29	−1.3	20.2	6.4	−3.3
Prices:	1934–40	1.0	12.2	6.2	1.0
	Average	−0.2	16.2	6.3	−1.2
Declining or	1942–45	2.5	26.1	4.5	−3.3
Moderate	1949–65	2.1	17.5	2.0	5.2
Inflation:	1981–84	3.9	16.8	20.0	13.1
	1985–90	3.5	20.3	14.5	5.5
	Average	2.5	20.1	8.8	5.0
Rapid	1940–47	6.8	12.3	2.6	8.6
Inflation:	1965–81	7.1	6.4	6.1	23.7
	Average	7.0	9.4	4.4	16.2

* As measured by the Consumer Price Index.

The fourth through sixth columns show how the various investment markets—stocks, bonds, and precious metals—performed given the different levels of inflation.

A quick glance at the results shows that stocks have performed worst during deflation. In fact, the period from 1929 to 1932 included one of the greatest market crashes in history.

The American economy, however, has not experienced deflation since the 1930s. How stocks performed the rest of the time has depended on the level of inflation. The proof is in the chart: When the multiyear trend for inflation is either low or moderate, stocks gain the most. Stocks do poorly when inflation is on the rise.

MEASURING INFLATION

By following inflation's cues, you can get out of stocks before they hit the skids and reenter the market when it has enormous potential for growth. The question is: How do you measure inflation?

The CPI is by far the most popular gauge (see above). This is the figure that newspeople and politicians glibly quote to prove their point.

Sometimes, the CPI is reported as a percentage increase from the previous month. Other times, the twelve-month rate of change is given. Some analysts follow what they call a core rate of inflation, which is the CPI's rate of change minus food and energy items.

My advice: The CPI does correlate with stock prices over long periods of time. But compared with some other inflation gauges, the CPI is a somewhat poor predictor for stocks.

One reason is that it's widely followed. Every time the CPI is released, the market reacts. A lower-than-expected rise never fails to bring a bullish response, a higher-than-expected rise a bearish response. If you try to time these swings, you'll usually come up empty-handed. Second, because the CPI includes many items, it changes only very slowly, making it tough to follow. And third, the CPI has an upward bias because consumer prices rarely go down. Companies seldom lower prices, unless forced to by their competitors.

Yet another popular way to measure inflation is the so-called GDP deflator. This is calculated quarterly and released at the same time as the figures for GDP (gross domestic product). GDP tries to measure America's total dollar output of goods and services over the latest three months. The GDP deflator shows what percentage of growth in the GDP is due simply to price increases.

Since GDP includes everything produced, the GDP deflator is easily the most comprehensive inflation gauge around. Unfortunately, it has several major pitfalls. For one, it's old news. Released only once every three months, it tells you about past rather than current trends. Moreover, the GDP deflator is based on thousands of estimates. So it's constantly revised, sometimes months after data are released.

Over the long term and after major revisions, the GDP deflator can be a good indicator of inflation trends. But in the near term, using it is like planning a vacation based on last season's weather. By the time you get the information, everything has changed.

GO TO THE SOURCE

To be useful, information on inflation must show trends as they're unfolding, rather than after they've happened. To get closer to the "source" of price trends, I track changes in producer prices, instead of the CPI or the GDP deflator. Unlike these two gauges, data on many producer prices are always available.

The most popular measure of producer prices is the Producer Price Index, or PPI. Like the CPI, the PPI is also calculated by the Labor Department and released once a month. Unlike the CPI, which concentrates on retail goods, the PPI measures prices of semifinished goods. As such, the PPI picks up changes in prices earlier than the CPI does.

As with the CPI, there are several ways to measure PPI. The best is the "all-commodity producer price index," which I call the "All Commodity PPI." This includes commodity prices, as well as prices of semifinished goods and finished goods that make up the PPI. So, the All Commodity PPI picks up changes in the overall inflation rate far more quickly than does PPI, CPI, or the GDP deflator.

Some well-known commodities are cotton, oil, grains, and so on. They are used in everything, so increases in their prices are eventually felt throughout the economy. For example, when oil prices rise the price of gasoline rises, and so does the price of plastic and other products that are made from petroleum. In addition, transportation costs rise. This, in turn, boosts the prices of products, from computers to cereal, that must be shipped.

Consumer prices will ultimately reflect changes in the prices of these "building blocks." But only long after the All Commodity PPI has reacted. And by then, stocks will probably have reacted as well.

The table on page 11 tells the story. It shows the relationship between stocks, as represented by the Standard and Poor's (S&P) 400, and the All Commodity PPI for the last seventy-five years.

As you can see, shifts in the All Commodity PPI usually occur before stock prices move. That's what makes the All Commodity PPI a good long-term measure of inflation.

STOCKS AND COMMODITY PRICES

ACPPI	S&P 400 12 Months Later
less than −2	+12.8
−2 to −1	+17.5
−1 to 0	+14.5
0 to 1	+13.4
1 to 3	+11.4
3 to 5	+4.5
greater than 5	+3.5

Twelve-month rate of change in All Commodity PPI, as a forecaster of S&P 400 twelve-month performance.

And because of this, the All Commodity PPI is the most reliable indicator for the long-term (three-to-five-year) future of the stock market.

TWO RULES

Looking at the period from September 1953 to the present, I discovered two specific patterns:

1. Whenever the All Commodity PPI has gained more than 3.5 percent annually on average over a five-year period, stocks have suffered. After the results are adjusted for inflation, stocks have gained only 1.7 percent during such periods.

This was the case from February 1973 through November 1985. During that time, the market fluctuated. But stocks in general were poor performers. Five-year bonds did just as well and provided very little of the anxiety and heartache that stock investors experienced during those tumultuous years.

2. Whenever the All Commodity PPI has gained less than 3.5 percent annually on average over a five-year period, stocks have done well. Their inflation-adjusted return during such times has been 10 percent. This was the case from September 1953 through January 1973, and again from December 1985 to the present.

If you buy and hold stocks when the All Commodity PPI is falling and sell when it's rising, you won't always reap big gains. But over the long haul, your money will grow and grow. To use this rule, you'll need to calculate a five-year moving average. That sounds complicated, but it's really not (see page 14 for step-by-step instructions).

IN THE INTERIM

For long-term stock forecasting, i.e., five years or more, the All Commodity PPI beats all other inflation gauges hands down. But what if you want to know how stocks will fare in the intermediate term, in other words, in the next one to three years?

To figure that out, I found, it's also necessary to take the Consumer Price Index (CPI) into account. I do this by subtracting the twelve-month rate of change in the All Commodity PPI from the twelve-month rate of change in the CPI.

The result is essentially a measure of corporate profit margins—the difference between companies' costs of production (as represented by the All Commodity PPI) and what they charge consumers (the CPI).

Profit margins reflect how profitable a firm is. The wider they are, the more profitable a company is and the greater its potential for earnings growth.

I've found that the difference between CPI and the All Commodity PPI is a remarkably reliable predictor of stock prices in the near term. The wider the difference, the better stocks are likely to perform.

For proof, look at the table "CPI-ACPPI and the S&P." As you can see, stocks do best when the CPI rate of change is at least five percentage points greater than the ACPPI rate of change.

The greater the gap—i.e., the higher the corporate margins—the better stocks have behaved over the next twelve months. But when the All Commodity PPI's rate of change has been at least five percentage points higher than that of the CPI, i.e., negative corporate margins, stocks have rung up negative returns.

CPI–ACPPI AND THE S&P

CPI–ACPPI	S&P 400 12 Months Later
greater than 5	25.7
3 to 5	17.3
2 to 3	11.6
0 to 2	8.6
−5 to 0	5.8
less than −5	−5.6

Difference between CPI and ACPPI twelve-month rates of change as a forecaster for S&P 400 twelve-month performance.

WHAT ABOUT THIS YEAR?

To really time the market, however, you've got to focus on how stocks are likely to fare in the next twelve months. In that case, using the All Commodity PPI on its own can actually trip you up.

In 1962, for example, the All Commodity PPI was in negative territory, but stocks declined over 25 percent from their January highs to their midyear lows. So following the All Commodity PPI alone would have been a disaster.

That's why raw inflation indicators like the All Commodity PPI are only a part of my forecasting model. You can't count on any one indicator to paint accurately the entire picture of the prospects for sustainable growth, at least not well enough for successfully timing the stock market one year out. In fact, they don't even tell the whole story when it comes to inflation.

To be a successful market timer for the twelve-month time frame, you've got to use other indicators, each of which is tightly connected to the trend in inflation. Together, they give a clear-cut picture of what lies ahead for the economy, and consequently, for stocks.

In the following chapter, I look at one such indicator—commodity prices. These don't include the costs of advertising, packaging, and transportation, which the All Commodity PPI does. They tend to react much more quickly than other indexes to underlying changes in the economy. As such, commodity prices are the rawest expression of inflation, and on their own are one of the strongest indicators around.

WORSHEET:
HOW TO CALCULATE CHANGES IN THE ALL COMMODITY PPI

To review, my rule for the All Commodity PPI is to buy and hold stocks when its five-year average rate of increase is less than 3.5 percent. I avoid stocks when the increase is greater. Here are the steps to follow to figure out this remarkably reliable indicator on your own:

1. Contact the U.S. Department of Labor, Bureau of Labor Statistics, Division of Industrial Prices and Price Indexes, Postal Square Building, Room 3840, 2 Massachusetts Ave. NE, Washington, DC 20212 (202-606-7705), and request a five-year record of producer prices. This report will include corresponding figures for the All Commodity Producer Price Index.

2. Find the annual rate of change for each of the past five years. For example, take the current index value and divide by the index value of a year ago. Subtract 1 from the result and multiply by 100 to find the annual percentage rate of change.

3. Find the average annual rate of change by adding together the percentage increases for each year and divide by five.

Here's an example of how to do these simple calculations:

1. Find the following index values:

    current value = 300
    value one year ago = 288
    value two years ago = 285
    value three years ago = 265
    value four years ago = 260
    value five years ago = 260

2. Do the following calculations:

    Divide 300 by 288 to get 1.042, or an annual rate of change of 4.2 percent.
    Divide 288 by 285 to get 1.011, or a rate of change of 1.1 percent.
    Divide 285 by 265 to get 1.076, or 7.6 percent.
    Divide 265 by 260 to arrive at 1.02, or 2.0 percent.
    Divide 260 by 260 to get 1.0, or a rate of change of 0 percent.

3. Add up all of the percentage change figures and divide by five to get an average five-year rate of increase of about 3.0 percent.

Your result of 3.0 percent indicates that the long-term trend for stocks is bullish. And because it's a five-year average, this figure smooths out yearly fluctuations. You can hang your hat on it!

Chapter 3 looks at unemployment insurance claims, which are the best measure of how much "slack" there is in the economy—i.e., how much it can grow without setting off inflationary warning signals.

Chapters 4 and 5 are concerned with interest rates and money supply indicators. Interest rates by themselves are overrated. But when put into the context of inflation, they can be excellent market forecasters.

My money supply indicators are not only a great warning system against rapid inflation. They're also the only indicator with a 100 percent perfect record for protecting you against infinitely more destructive deflation.

Chapter 6 is concerned with price-to-earnings ratios, or P/Es. By themselves, these are very poor market-timing tools. But when put into the context of long-term inflation, they have a perfect record for predicting both bull and bear markets. Finally, in Chapter 7, I put all of the indicators together into a coherent strategy for stock market success.

In each chapter I show you two things: first, the relationship between each individual indicator and stocks' performance over the years; second, the relationship between each indicator and stocks, when put into the context of current inflation.

For each indicator, I give you a reliable trading rule for following it alone. But as you read, you'll discover that the indicators work best when we put them all together. That's the subject of Chapter 7.

A great general once said that the secret of battlefield success is to "know one's enemy." In the stock market, inflation is that enemy. Inflation affects everything in the stock market. Even if that's all you learn from reading this book, you'll never be melted down in market crashes, and you'll reap big profits from stocks for as long as you live. Knowing inflation is the key to stock market success.

POINTS TO REMEMBER

1. The stock market looks ahead, never behind. Economic growth must be sustainable in the future if stocks are to rise.
2. If inflation is rising, growth is not sustainable. Stocks will fall. If inflation is falling, growth is sustainable. Stocks will rise.
3. The best measure of long-term inflation trends is the five-year average annual rate of change in the All Commodity Producer Price Index (ACPPI). You can get data for it from the Labor Department by calling 202-606-7705.
4. The wider the difference between the twelve-month rates of change in ACPPI and the CPI, the better stocks are likely to perform.
5. Chapters 2 through 6 describe the indicators that form the building blocks of my forecasting model. All are based on the same relationship discussed in this chapter—rising inflation is bearish, falling inflation bullish for stocks.

2

Commodity Prices: Closest to a Sure Thing

LET ME LAY IT ON THE LINE AGAIN. Inflation is without doubt the best stock market forecaster. And when it comes to forecasting the next twelve months for stocks, the best indicator of inflation is commodity prices.

One reason I tip my hat to commodity prices is that they're never revised once they've been made public. So, I can count on them. But they also have one more amazing thing going for them. Compared with all other indicators, they're the most closely related to moves in inflation.

As we saw in Chapter 1, bull markets hinge on the economy's ability to grow without igniting inflation. Once inflation is a threat, you can kiss both growth and stocks good-bye.

Commodity prices are the simplest, rawest expression of inflation. That's because they're the basic building blocks of all that's produced—the fuels, metals, paper, and grains and other foodstuffs that are refined, grounded, pounded, and packaged into life's luxuries and necessities.

So when commodity prices rise, so does the cost of myriad other products and services in ricochet fashion. Inflation then flares up across the board and burns out economic growth: the bull market in stocks is sure to end.

A rise in the price of oil, for example, eventually makes gasoline more expensive, so transportation costs also go up. This, in turn, boosts prices of everything that's shipped, from food to computers to cars.

Likewise, higher grain prices raise the cost of cereal and bread. And

17

because livestock depend on grains, meat becomes more expensive, too.

You don't have to go back any further than the 1970s to see the awesome power of commodity prices over stocks. During that decade, prices of scores of commodities—from oil to grains—soared. The stock market scored one of its worst performances ever during this decade, losing an average of 1.3 percent per year, if returns are adjusted for inflation.

Stop and think about that. Had you bought a basket of stocks (the S&P 500) at the end of 1969, and held them through the end of 1979, you'd be in the hole 14 percent in real terms, even including dividends paid.

But look what happened in the 1980s, when commodity prices generally trended down. Stocks gained an average of 11 percent a year, adjusted for inflation. That was one of the best showings ever for any financial asset.

The bottom line: When commodity prices are stable to downtrending, you can even take a round-the-world trip and not have to worry about your stocks. Indeed, your investments are likely to pay for the vacation!

WHICH COMMODITIES?

As you can see, commodity prices dramatically influence the stock market. The degree to which they do depends on how much they rise or fall as a group.

With the possible exception of oil, price rises in a single commodity usually have very little effect on stocks. For example, from April 1988 to April 1989, copper prices doubled, partly in response to rumors about a supply interruption from the Chilean mines. But inflation remained at bay, and stocks actually rose 14 percent during that time (more than 17 percent if you count dividends).

For commodity prices to really boost inflation (to have a truly negative effect on stocks), they must rise across the board. In other words, prices of most commodities must be rising.

The best way to gauge the trend in commodity prices is to look at an index of various commodity prices. That way, spectacular increases in the price of one commodity will be put into context by how others fared.

On Wall Street, the most popular index for measuring commodity prices is the Commodity Research Bureau's (CRB) futures index. The CRB's index is a composite of the prices of futures contracts for some twenty-one different commodities, ranging from pork bellies to orange juice.

I have two major qualms with this index. First, futures contracts are rights to buy or sell a certain quantity of a commodity at a specified price before a set date. As such they reflect investors' beliefs about the future direction of commodity prices, as well as current prices.

Most important, the CRB 21 includes some commodities whose prices don't have a big impact on the economy. As a result, a move in this index may not be significant, unless the right commodities are at the root of it.

That's why I use a lesser-known offshoot of the CRB index: the CRB Bureau of Labor Statistics (BLS) spot industrial price index. Unlike the CRB, the BLS index reflects only "spot" prices—what commodities cost now.

And the BLS index weeds out commodities with only a marginal effect on the economy. The result is an index of just thirteen commodities, each with a strong and proven effect on the economy.

BLS INDUSTRIAL COMMODITIES

Burlap
Copper scrap
Cotton
Hides, heavy native
Lead scrap, heavy soft
Print cloth
Rosin, window glass
Rubber, No. 1 ribbed smoked sheets
Steel scrap, No. 1
Tallow, prime
Tin, grade A
Wool tops (nominal)
Zinc, prime western

The BLS index is one of the best market timing tools around. Like the unemployment insurance claims indicator discussed in the next chapter, it can help you beat the pants off the Wall Street pros by following it and it alone.

When the BLS index talks, the market usually doesn't listen right away. But when this guage rises dramatically, inflation is almost always just around the corner. And usually, stocks are about to take it on the chin. On the other hand, if the BLS index is slipping, stocks are usually getting ready to tear up the track.

The key to making good use of the BLS is determining how much the index has risen or fallen in percentage terms over the past twelve months. To calculate a percentage change for a twelve-month period, simply divide the most recent figure by the figure for twelve months ago and subtract from the result. Note that you don't have to go back twelve months exactly. For example, using a six- or even a four-month rate of change, the results would be about as strong. Even rates of change up to eighteen months work pretty well.

Not every percentage move in the BLS index creates an equal and opposite move in stocks. But generally, when the BLS index has dropped over the past twelve months, the stock market can look ahead to a good year.

Lower commodity prices mean little upward pressure on prices in general, hence little inflation. And with inflation at bay, stocks have almost never failed to respond positively.

Conversely, whenever the BLS index has posted a significant rise from year-ago levels—30 percent or more—the result has almost always been a downer for stocks. The reason: Higher commodity prices have set off a rise in economy-wide inflation, which is always the death knell for stocks.

Take a look at our table, "A Very Accurate Indicator," which shows the relationship between the S&P 400 stock index and the BLS index. Sharply rising commodity prices are perhaps the best warning signal that inflation is on the way back. More often than not, it's time to get out of stocks.

The most bearish time has been when commodity prices have risen more than 40 percent over a twelve-month period. Since World War

A VERY ACCURATE INDICATOR

BLS	S&P 400
more than 40%	−21.9%
30 to 40	−0.2%
20 to 30	+1.6%
10 to 20	+4.4%
5 to 10	+7.2%
0 to 5	+4.1%
−5 to 0	+6.9%
−10 to −5	+16.3%
−10 to −20	+24.1%
less than −20	+6.3%

Twelve-month change in the BLS industrial commodity price index as a forecaster for S&P 400 twelve-month performance.

II, there has been a total of eleven months when this was the case. Had you bought stocks at any point during those times, you would have lost an average of 22 percent over the next twelve months.

The only exception was May 1974 to May 1975. But then the gain was less than 1 percent. Plus to realize that gain you would have had to stomach more than a 30 percent drop first.

Stocks also do poorly when the twelve-month rise in commodity prices is in the 30 to 40 percent range. The last time this happened was in the twelve months ending September 1987. Then, the BLS was off to the races to the tune of a 34 percent rise. That played a big role in stocks' massive 30 percent crash that fall.

When the twelve-month rise in commodity prices is between 0 and 20 percent, however, trouble does not necessarily lie ahead for stocks. It's natural for commodity prices to rise in an economy that's growing. If other conditions for low inflation that we'll discuss in later chapters are in place, rising commodity prices may not lead to widespread inflation. This means stocks can actually keep rising. This happened in the mid-1980s and in the mid-1950s. From February 1954 to February 1955, for example, stocks advanced over 40 percent, even while commodity prices rose about 12 percent.

When commodity prices are falling or stable over a twelve-month period, it's almost always been a great time to hold stocks. That's because falling prices are a sign that the economy can keep growing without inflation flaring up. The bull market is alive and kicking.

Consider what happened from May 1985 to May 1986. Then, collapsing prices for oil and other commodities sent stocks up over 30 percent. Following commodities' lead would have been the no-brainer way to get rich quick.

The most bullish time is when commodity prices have slipped between 10 and 20 percent. The BLS index has dropped this much sixty-eight times since World War II. On average, stocks have soared 24 percent over the next year.

Out of these sixty-eight instances, stocks posted a loss in only two twelve-month intervals: from September 1952 to September 1953, and from October 1952 to October 1953. And as it turned out, this rocky time was simply a prelude to one of the greatest bull markets of this century. Sooner or later the effect of falling commodity prices always works its magic on stocks.

The only exception to this rule is when truly deflationary conditions exist in the economy. However, this has not been a problem since the Great Depression. Back then, big drops in commodity prices were a symptom of huge cuts in industrial production. There was a lot of room in the economy for noninflationary growth. But other factors, such as a shrinking money supply (see Chapter 5), were keeping the economy on the ropes.

Still, our table shows that too much of a good thing—falling commodity prices—is usually not so good. Notice that when prices fall more than 20 percent in twelve months, stocks' gains are considerably less than when the year-over-year change is in the optimum range of −10 to −20 percent. Again, falling—not plummeting—commodity prices are what's best for stocks.

MY TRADING RULE

I have a very simple rule when it comes to using commodity prices to trade stocks for twelve-month gains: I buy and hold stocks whenever the BLS has fallen at least 5 percent over the prior twelve months.

I head for the exits when the BLS gains at least 10 percent over a twelve-month period.

My strategy works beautifully despite the gray areas I mentioned above: the negative results of plummeting commodity prices, as well as the sometimes positive effects of rising commodity prices, provided other conditions for noninflationary growth exist.

The table below shows the fruits of my labor. Since the 1950s, my rule has issued a buy signal over a total of 257 months. Had you held stocks during these periods, your average annual gain would have been nearly 25 percent, close to 30 percent counting dividends.

Indeed, during the thirty or so years in which the rate of change in commodity prices was outside my buy and hold range, stocks lost ground. You just aren't going to find a simple strategy that works better than this.

The relationship between commodity prices and the stock market is so strong that a number of other trading rules can work equally well. I've also charted a "−5 percent (buy)/+5 percent (sell)" trading strategy, and the results are not much different.

If you keep careful tabs on the BLS index and follow my −5/+10

RECORD OF MY TRADING RULE

Number of Months Invested in Stocks	Action in S&P 400	Percentage Gains in S&P 400
Oct 51 to Feb 55 (40)	23.80 to 38.06	59.9%
Apr 57 to Apr 59 (24)	48.08 to 60.92	26.7
Nov 60 to Aug 64 (45)	58.89 to 86.70	47.2
Oct 66 to May 69 (31)	82.01 to 114.50	39.6
Oct 70 to May 72 (19)	92.85 to 120.20	29.5
Dec 74 to Jun 76 (18)	74.80 to 114.50	53.1
Jun 80 to Aug 83 (34)	128.80 to 183.16	42.2
Dec 84 to Apr 87 (28)	183.62 to 335.43	82.7
Jan 90 to Jul 91 (18)	390.58 to 452.92	16.0
257		24.8*

Results of trading strategy of buying stocks when commodity prices have fallen at least 5 percent over the past 12 months, and selling after they have risen at least 10 percent over the past 12 months.

* Compounded Average Annual Gain.

percent rule, you'll almost always come out a winner. Here's how to get the numbers, step-by-step:

1. Find the value of the BLS spot price index. Monthly figures can be found in the *Survey of Current Business*, page C-3, series 23, "Index of Spot Market Prices, Raw Industrial Materials." To order, see Appendix, page 183. For weekly data (not essential) the Commodity Research Bureau publishes a *Commodity Index Report* for $225/year. To order call 800-621-5271.

2. Find the closing value of the BLS index twelve months before the latest value. This is available in the *Survey of Current Business*.

3. Subtract the year-ago value from the current value and divide by the year-ago value. Multiply by 100 to find the percentage rate of change. For example, if the BLS was at 280 last year and 308 now, the rate of change is +10 percent $(308-280) \div 280 \times 100$.

4. If the rate of change is less than +10 percent, the bull market should have enough juice to keep going for at least the next twelve months.

If you get close to +10, monitor the rate of change closely. Should it tick up to 11 percent, for example, the odds of stock market success over the next twelve months decrease substantially. Before making any moves, be sure to check the table "A Very Accurate Indicator" on page 20 to see how the market has performed given various readings on the BLS.

DON'T BE SLICKERED

There's one more thing you must know about commodities. Rapidly rising oil prices can have a catastrophic effect on stocks in the short term, even if prices of other commodities are falling.

But as long as prices of other commodities don't follow oil's rise, the impact of more expensive oil will be temporary, and the bull market should resume within months. Remember: It takes more than a rise in just one commodity, even if it's oil, to make inflation a threat to sustainable economic growth.

Oil is the single most important commodity in the modern world. It provides more than half of America's energy, and it's used in a wide variety of other products, from plastics to fertilizers.

So oil prices have a far greater effect on the economy than do prices of other commodities. In fact, rising oil prices have often triggered rises in commodity prices across the board, setting off major waves of inflation.

During the 1970s, skyrocketing oil prices were at the root of the double-digit inflation. And several times in recent years—most notably following Iraq's invasion of Kuwait—oil prices have exploded, setting off fears of a repeat of the 1970s.

Oil's ability to affect stocks, even when other commodity prices are falling, is compounded by the political volatility of places like the Middle East and the former Soviet Union, where oil is bought. The market hates uncertainty. And when oil supplies are threatened by political events, stocks usually sell off sharply.

Consequently, when oil rises, stocks tend to fall. When oil falls, stocks rise. And the effect is almost immediate.

When Iraq invaded Kuwait in August 1990, for example, the market saw an immediate threat to world oil supplies. Oil prices doubled in a matter of weeks. Fear of soaring inflation turned a stock market retreat into a rout, with stocks losing more than 20 percent in only eight weeks or so.

Fortunately, prices of other commodities failed to follow oil's upward thrust in the latter half of 1990. From August 1, 1990, through January 1, 1991, the BLS index actually fell by about 6 percent, despite the fact that oil prices had more than doubled.

Because other commodities refused to follow oil's lead, inflation never had a chance to get off the ground. Once the furor about oil died down, sustainable economic growth and the bull market in stocks resumed. But few investors caught on to this fact before it was too late. In mid-January 1991, the United States began its bombardment of Baghdad, and oil prices were cut almost in half. The stock market soared more than 20 percent in the next eight weeks.

INFLATION'S NOT EVERYTHING

I can't overemphasize the importance of inflation for determining stocks' future. Understanding how inflation works and keeping an eye on it are vital to your stock market success.

To review, the best indicator to monitor the long-term (three-to-five-year) health of the stock market is the five-year moving average of the All Commodity Producer Price Index's (ACPPI) rate of change. The best indicator for the intermediate term (one to three years) is the difference between the twelve-month rates of change of the ACPPI and Consumer Price Index. Finally, the best indicator for the twelve-month future of stocks is the BLS index.

If you follow the indicators according to the rules I've laid down in the first two chapters of this book, you'll beat the pants off the market's pros every time.

There's nothing mystical about it. It's just that simple. Inflation explains most of the fluctuation in the market. In a world where investors flock to faddish nonsense like Kondratieff Waves and Gann Cycles, simply paying heed to these obvious signals will give you an enormous advantage.

But just as with the other indicators described in this book, commodities don't tell the whole story. If you use them in conjunction with the other indicators in this book, you can improve your returns radically.

POINTS TO REMEMBER

1. When commodity prices rise rapidly year over year, it's bearish for stocks' twelve-month outlook. When commodity prices fall year over year, it's bullish for stocks.
2. The best measure of commodity price trends is the twelve-month rate of change in the BLS spot industrial price index. You can get

figures for the BLS weekly from the Commodity Research Bureau, and monthly from the *Survey of Current Business*.

3. Our trading rule for using commodity prices alone as an indicator is to buy when the BLS index has fallen at least 5 percent over the prior twelve months. Sell when it gains at least 10 percent.

3

Unemployment:
Why Bad News Is Good News

WHEN UNEMPLOYMENT IS FALLING, most people greet the news with a cheer. But smart investors start to watch their stocks like hawks.

That's because when it comes to unemployment, good news is often bad news for stocks. If you don't follow me yet, you're not alone. Most investors think that rising employment is good news for stocks because it means the economy is growing.

But as I showed in the first chapter of this book, stock prices are always based on expectations for future growth, not what's happening now. When things are really good, i.e., unemployment is falling, economic growth is running at close to its top rate.

So, the potential for future growth is less than at any other time. The stock market, anticipating the next downturn, inevitably starts to fall. Conversely, when unemployment is high, things are bad and bound to get better; stocks rally and keep going up.

Through bitter experience, the investment pros have learned that economic booms follow busts and vice versa. The prosperity of the late 1970s, for example, was followed by the recession of the early 1980s. And the recovery of the mid-1980s was followed by the slump of the early 1990s.

Let's revisit mid-1987 again. At that time, one of the biggest signs that the economy was overheating, or nearing an inflationary stage, was very low unemployment. More people were working in 1987 than at any time since the economic recovery began in 1982. So, although inflation does the best job of signaling when economic growth has peaked (see Chapter 1), unemployment ranks a close second.

MY TWO RULES

Rule 1: *When Unemployment Is Trending Down Sharply* (just how much, I'll show you later), *Avoid Stocks.*

The table on page 30 shows the unemployment rate at every major stock market peak since World War II. Notice that when stocks reach a top, unemployment is lower than it was 12 months earlier—in almost every case. Typically, the faster unemployment is falling, the farther stocks eventually tumble.

Look at the figures for 1987. Back then, unemployment had dropped to an eight-year low. During a single week in October 1987, stocks took one of their worst blood baths. And they didn't fully recover until 1989, when unemployment started rising again.

Rule 2: *When Unemployment Is Climbing, the Stock Market Is a Good Place to Be.*

By the winter of 1982, for example, unemployment had staged an alarming rise to nearly 11 percent. The upshot: Stocks posted one of the greatest rallies in history, shooting up 60 percent in the next nine months. For smaller equities, triple and quadruple gains were not uncommon.

One of the most dramatic examples of my rule 2 occurred in the beginning of 1991. Then, unemployment was rising at a rate not seen since the bleak days of 1982.

This horrible news appeared to confirm the down-and-out attitude of bigwig money managers, from Marty Zweig to Allen Sinai. Some of these guys were talking not just about recession, but about the big *D*: Depression. Almost everyone was selling stocks and loading up on cash.

Somehow, these very intelligent and experienced folks overlooked the fact that bull markets thrive on really bad news. Sure enough, the Dow Jones Industrial Average and other market indexes gained about 20 percent between mid-January and March 1991. Smaller stocks staged one of their biggest rallies this century.

UNEMPLOYMENT AT MARKET TOPS

Market Top	Market Decline*	Unemployment Rate	Year-Earlier Unemployment Rate
January 1953	−15.9%	2.9%	3.2%
July 1957	−21.2	4.2	4.4
July 1959	−15.2	5.1	7.5
December 1961	−28.5	6.0	6.6
January 1966	−22.3	4.0	4.9
December 1968	−35.8	3.4	3.8
January 1973	−48.3	4.9	5.8
September 1976	−21.0	7.6	3.4
November 1980	−29.1	7.5	5.9
October 1983	−13.1	8.8	10.4
August 1987	−35.0	6.0	6.9

* Top to bottom decline in Standard & Poor's 400.

UNEMPLOYMENT AND INFLATION

Think again of the economy as a train; its engine's temperature gauge is the employment rate. In the middle of a recession, when employment is relatively low, the train is just starting to leave the station and its engine is cool, in other words, inflation is low.

But the faster the economic train is going, the more people start working. The pool of available workers dries up, and this means higher wages, which will probably be passed on to the consumer. Prices rise, causing workers to ask for still-higher wages, and so on. The bottom line: rapidly falling unemployment typically brings on inflation.

The Federal Reserve, the train's chief engineer, is likely to hit the brakes when inflation starts rising. It does this by pushing up interest rates. At this point, the stock market is likely to peak.

Only after growth has slowed markedly and unemployment is again high will the stock market be ready for another move up. That's because at that point the Fed is likely to step on the accelerator—lower interest rates—to get the train moving.

Consider what happened from 1982 to 1984. The first three quarters of 1982 were a recession; unemployment was surging. To revive the economy, the Fed stepped on the accelerator. From early 1982 to early 1983, short-term interest rates were cut nearly in half. The Dow Jones Industrial Average soared by nearly 60 percent in the next nine months.

By year-end 1983, unemployment had fallen from 10.8 percent to 8.3 percent. Reflecting this, inflation had climbed from a low of 2.5 percent to nearly 4 percent. To combat inflation, the central bank stepped on the brakes—hiked short-term interest rates. Stocks peaked in the autumn and in the next nine months fell by about 15 percent.

As you can see, the unemployment rate is an important early warning gauge for measuring whether inflation is becoming a threat, or if it's on the fade. That's why unemployment is such a useful indicator for judging where stocks are headed. But just as with measuring inflation, you must be careful about where you get your employment numbers.

GAUGES THAT LIE

At 8:30 A.M. on the second Friday of every month, the U.S. Department of Labor releases two figures for the prior month: (1) the unemployment rate, which is followed by the mass media; and (2) payroll employment, on which the Federal Reserve keeps an eye.

Both of these stats have a large popular following. But both are seriously flawed from an investor's point of view.

The unemployment rate tries to measure the number of jobless people looking for work as a percentage of the total workforce. You've probably heard the result cited on the Friday evening news or seen it in your local paper on Saturday morning. Every politician, financial reporter, and TV anchorman knows this stat and quotes it ad nauseam.

But not even trained economists know how to tell what level of employment will cause the economic train to overheat. The upshot: The unemployment rate is practically useless from an investor's point of view. Rather than try to base an investment strategy on this figure, leave it to the politicians.

PAYROLL DOESN'T PAY

Payroll employment, the other popular measure, tries to gauge the total number of working Americans. The Federal Reserve and many analysts monitor the results to determine if the economy is growing at the "right" speed.

Although it's usually listed in the same newspaper article as the unemployment rate, payroll employment is rarely mentioned by the media. You'll have to dig into the text to find it.

My advice is not to bother; the results can't be trusted. That's because payroll employment figures are based on estimates and are often revised dramatically.

The process works like this. State agencies mail about 350,000 surveys to representative nonagricultural businesses to find out how many people are working for them. Based on the results, each agency gives statewide estimates to the Labor Department, which compiles the data into a single figure.

But survey data results are never complete when figures are released. As more data roll in, still more revisions must be made.

The difference between initial and revised figures can border on the ludicrous. In February 1987, for example, the Labor Department reported that January payroll employment had climbed by 5.4 percent. After final revisions, the gain was reduced to only 2.7 percent. Worse, revisions like this are the rule rather than the exception.

Imagine if you had to make similar revisions when charting your son or daughter's growth rate. You'd be overestimating the increase in the size clothes they need by twofold.

Incredibly, many market traders do exactly that. They sell stocks on a large upmove in payroll employment only to buy back when the figures are later revised and the actual gain is somewhat smaller. Most of them end up driving taxis.

Because of these problems, the best idea is to ignore completely the Labor Department's monthly report. Instead, concentrate on a more obscure but infinitely more reliable piece of data: unemployment insurance claims.

TOP JOB INDICATOR

Initial state unemployment insurance claims tell you how many people have filed for state unemployment insurance for the first time all across America. This figure is released weekly by the Labor Department, every Thursday morning at 8:30.

Claims provide the most reliable information about the labor market. Because the results are based on raw data, not surveys, they've never been revised significantly. Once figures are released, you can count on them.

And unlike the unemployment rate, the number of claims does not require interpretation. If they're rising consistently, the economy is slowing down. Fewer claims signal that economic growth is speeding up.

Still, unemployment insurance claims are one of the most obscure pieces of data around. Few local papers report them. Even *Barron's* excludes them from its "Market Laboratory." And *The Harper-Collins Dictionary of Economics*, a commonly used text with more than 1700 entries and diagrams, makes no mention of them whatsoever. Nor will you find them in most standard economic textbooks.

The main reason most analysts ignore unemployment insurance claims is that weekly figures tend to fluctuate wildly due to seasonal factors. For example, for the week ended December 28, 1990, claims were 396,000. But the next week they were 472,000. (The weekly results are listed in the Friday edition of *The Wall Street Journal*, or your broker can get them for you by tuning in to a popular news recall service, such as Dow Jones or Reuters.)

Granted, if you follow claims weekly, it's tough to spot a trend. It's like trying to measure major changes in climate by checking the thermometer every week.

Monthly averages of unemployment insurance claims, however, smooth out the weekly aberrations. For example, the average claims for December 1990 and January 1991 were 455,000. The monthly results provide a crystal clear picture of the long-term trend.

One way to get a monthly average is to add up the last four weekly figures for unemployment insurance claims and divide by 4. Another way is to wait until *The Wall Street Journal* publishes an average of the previous month's weekly figures for claims. Sometime during the fourth week of February, for example, an average for January claims is released.

This figure won't be quite as timely as adding up and averaging figures each week. But results are virtually the same because the trend in claims changes very slowly. When predicting moves in the stock market, a month's delay in the figures normally won't make a bit of difference.

The best way to spot a trend in unemployment insurance claims is to look at changes from the previous year. For example, compare January 1991 average weekly claims with January 1990 figures.

FINE-TUNING

The most important thing to keep in mind is: The greater the year-over-year increase in unemployment insurance claims, the higher stocks are likely to go. Our table "Big Claims, Big Gains" shows how greater increases in claims correspond with greater boosts in stocks. For example, whenever the year-over-year rise in claims has been

BIG CLAIMS, BIG GAINS

Initial State Unemployment Insurance Claims	Average Year-over-Year Change in S&P 400
Greater than +60%	+30.7%
+40 to +60	+24.2
+20 to +40	+17.4
+10 to +20	+12.1
0 to 10	+4.9
−10 to 0	+8.4
Less than −10	+1.7

12-month changes in unemployment insurance claims and Standard & Poor's performance for the following 12 months.

above 60 percent, stocks were up an average of 30.7 percent twelve months later.

Buying stocks when unemployment insurance claims have increased more than 60 percent is a sure thing. You could literally buy stocks and then take a year-long world cruise, secure in the knowledge that your vacation would be paid for when you returned.

The absolute worst the market has done after such an increase in claims is a 10.4 percent gain in May 1975. The best was an off-the-chart 47 percent gain in July 1954.

Of course, unemployment insurance claims rarely increase that much from year to year. In fact, they've done it in only twenty-one months out of the last forty years. The trick is to find a rate of increase in claims that can reliably tip you off to bull markets, and which occurs often enough to be useful.

THE 15 PERCENT RULE

One good trading guide I use is what I call the 15 percent rule. Stocks will almost always outperform other investments whenever unemployment insurance claims have increased 15 percent or more from the prior year.

The table "The 15 Percent Rule" shows the results of buying and holding stocks whenever the year-over-year increase in claims has been above 15 percent. Sell whenever this is no longer true. Columns one and two show the period and number of months, respectively, that the year-over-year increase in claims was more than 15 percent. Column four shows the average annual gain (or loss) in stocks during that time.

Since the early 1950s, this system has flashed ten buy signals, or about one every two to three years. Nine of these ten times, stocks rose. On average, stocks scored a hefty average annual gain of 18.1 percent, not including dividends. Compare that to the mere 7.8 percent a buy-and-hold strategy would have netted.

More often than not, gains from using my 15 percent rule would have been over 20 percent. From November 1953 to January 1955, for example, stocks shot up more than 50 percent. More recently,

THE 15 PERCENT RULE

From	Number of Months	S&P 400 From	Percent Change
November 1953 to January 1955	14	24.51 to 36.79	50.1%
November 1957 to December 1958	13	43.41 to 57.09	31.5
June 1960 to August 1961	14	61.06 to 71.69	17.4
May 1967 to August 1961	4	99.59 to 103.80	4.2
February 1970 to May 1971	15	95.73 to 112.40	17.4
February 1974 to December 1975	22	104.10 to 99.31	−4.7
November 1979 to December 1980	13	116.10 to 152.20	31.1
January 1982 to January 1983	12	131.08 to 162.02	23.6
November 1989 to June 1990	7	395 to 417.00	5.4
October 1990 to October 1991	2	369.35 to 457.39	23.8
Annual Gain for 114 Months in the Market			18.1%
Annual Gain from Buy-and-Hold Strategy 1953–1991			7.8%

from October 1990 to October 1991, stocks rang up an annual gain of 23.8 percent. And you would have avoided every major bear market during the period.

To dramatize this relationship even more, suppose you acted contrary to this rule, buying only when unemployment insurance claims were falling by more than 15 percent. In other words, buying on good news.

The table "Good News Is Bad News" shows how you would have done. You would have been in the market for a total of 6.25 years, for an average annual loss of 2.8 percent. A dollar's worth of assets invested in 1953 would have shrunk to less than 83 cents. The biggest loss would have come in 1987, when the market collapsed 22.6 percent.

Incidentally, unemployment claims were falling more than 15 percent a year in September 1987. That was a sure-fire sign that inflation was in an uptrend and that the current level of economic growth was unsustainable. And that was a major reason I suspected stocks were about to crash, and take the real estate market down with them.

GOOD NEWS IS BAD NEWS

From	Number of Months	S&P 400 From	Percent Change
January 1953 to April 1953	3	26.45 to 24.84	−6.1%
July 1953 to October 1953	3	24.41 to 23.96	−1.8
March 1955 to March 1956	12	37.65 to 50.59	34.4
March 1959 to November 1959	8	59.79 to 61.46	2.8
December 1961 to August 1962	8	75.29 to 61.29	−19.2
December 1965 to March 1966	3	97.66 to 95.04	−2.7
May 1966 to August 1966	3	92.85 to 86.40	−6.9
September 1966 to November 1966	2	83.11 to 86.10	3.6
May 1968 to September 1968	4	107.00 to 110.50	3.3
October 1972 to January 1973	3	122.40 to 132.60	8.3
January 1976 to September 1976	8	108.50 to 118.20	8.9
June 1981 to October 1981	4	148.70 to 134.00	−9.9
June 1983 to August 1984	14	187.41 to 186.86	−0.3
September 1987 to January 1988	4	372.49 to 288.36	−22.6
Cumulative Value of $1 for 75 Months in Market			0.83
Average Annual Loss			−2.8

That's why I was so adamant that my friends should take that first offer on their vacation home!

GETTING RESULTS

As I've said, figures for weekly and monthly unemployment insurance claims are tough to get. But once you find them, their relative obscurity works nicely to your advantage.

Changes in the widely publicized unemployment rate or payroll employment data routinely cause short-term fits and starts in the market. Nobody reacts that way to unemployment insurance claims. The Thursday morning report is not even picked up by most of the media. As a result, you have a nice lead time to act whenever the results change.

Below is a review of how to find and use unemployment insurance claims:

1. Get the most recent monthly average of initial state unemployment insurance claims. The best source for this is either *The Wall Street Journal* or the *Survey of Current Business* (page C-1, series 5). They're listed as "Average Weekly Initial Claims for Unemployment Insurance."

Typically the *Journal* publishes data for the prior month sometime during the last week of the current month. For example, during the fourth week of February, an average for January claims would be released. Many libraries carry back issues of *The Wall Street Journal* on microfiche.

2. Find the monthly average of unemployment insurance claims for the same month a year ago. For example, if the most recent figures you have are for July 1993, find the figures for July 1992.

You can get unemployment insurance claims for prior months from the Department of Commerce Business Statistics summaries and supplements, found in most libraries. Also the *Survey of Current Business* publishes the most recent year of data in each issue.

This publication also includes data for other indicators—money supply, commodity prices, and P/Es—that I discuss throughout this book. To order, see Appendix, page 183.

3. Subtract the prior year's average unemployment insurance claims from the current year's. Divide the result by the prior year's to find the annual percentage rate of change in claims. If the most recent month for claims is March 1993, subtract March 1992 figures from it and divide the result by March 1992 figures.

For example, suppose average March 1993 unemployment insurance claims were 375,000. If March 1992 average claims were 350,000, the year-over-year increase in claims is 25,000. By dividing, you find a percentage gain of 7.1 percent ([25,000 ÷ 350,000] × 100).

4. Compare your results with how stocks have performed during similar rates of change in claims. Using our example above, a 7.1 percent rise in unemployment insurance claims is less than what our 15 percent rule says is bullish for stocks.

A quick look back at the table "Big Claims, Big Gains" reveals the average gain for stocks at that level of claims is only 4.9 percent. Therefore, though stocks would probably rise, chances are you'd want to avoid a big commitment to the market.

On the other hand, if March 1993 reported an average of 410,000 claims, the percentage increase in unemployment insurance claims would be 17.1 percent (410,000 − 350,000) ÷ 350,000). Since this is greater than our 15 percent rule, you'd definitely want to be in there buying stocks.

ALL TOGETHER

As a single indicator, unemployment insurance claims have an excellent record in correctly forecasting the stock market one year out, all by themselves. Following them alone, you can ring up strong returns, nine times out of ten.

But like any other indicator, unemployment insurance claims are not 100 percent effective. From February 1974 to December 1975, for example, stocks fell while claims were rising more than 15 percent a year. Several other times, the market rose but managed only subpar gains. And once, from March 1955 to March 1956, our rule for unemployment insurance claims completely missed a 34.4 percent gain in stocks.

Claims failed to forecast the future during those times because other factors outweighed the effect of unemployment on inflation. In the 1970s, for example, oil and other commodity prices were raging out of control. As a result, stocks fell even though unemployment was rising.

In the mid-1950s, conversely, the aftermath of the Korean War sent producer price inflation into freefall. The economy had plenty of room to grow without igniting inflation, despite low unemployment.

Always remember that the employment picture, though very important, is only one building block that makes the market tick. That's why unemployment insurance claims should always be used in conjunction with the other indicators described in this book, especially the inflation indicators described in the first two chapters.

But if you follow unemployment insurance claims' lead, you'll be way ahead of the crowd. And the next time Wall Street and the press fret about the employment scene, you'll be ready to take advantage of it.

POINTS TO REMEMBER

1. Rising unemployment is bullish for stocks, because it means the economy has room for sustainable growth without igniting inflation. Falling unemployment is bearish, because it means the economy is rapidly approaching the limits of sustainable growth, and inflation is a threat.
2. The best measure of unemployment is the twelve-month rate of change in initial unemployment insurance claims. The higher the rate of change, the more bullish for stocks. Falling or negative rates of change are bearish for stocks.
3. Buy stocks when claims are rising faster than 15 percent, year over year. Sell when the rate of change slips below that. You can find data for unemployment insurance claims by reading *The Wall Street Journal* or from the *Survey of Current Business*.

4

Interest Rates: Fact and Fiction

WHENEVER I'M AT A GET-TOGETHER, be it an investment conference or a dinner party, people always ask me where interest rates are headed.

This is understandable. Interest rates, after all, are the price we all pay to borrow. And borrowing is one of the things that make the world go around. Businesses borrow to expand, you and I borrow to buy houses and cars, and Uncle Sam borrows to fund social programs.

But the main reason interest rates are so enthusiastically studied is that they have a decent record of forecasting stock market swings, at least on the face of it. To hear many in the media talk, every flip and twist in stocks is directly caused by changes in interest rates. Millions of investors watch other indicators, such as inflation and unemployment, only to figure out where interest rates are headed.

Some of the avid attention paid to interest rates is deserved. Most of the time, falling interest rates go hand in hand with higher stock prices. And more striking, stocks have never suffered when both short- and long-term rates were lower than they were the year before.

Look at the two tables, "Two So-So Indicators." As you can see, when interest rates have fallen steeply, stocks have generally risen. Whenever short-term interest rates have dropped more than 20 percent over twelve months, the stock market has risen considerably. And whenever long-term interest rates have dropped more than 10 percent over a twelve-month period, big rises in stocks have resulted.

This may seem like an impressive record at first. But if you flip back to the last two chapters, you'll see it really doesn't stack up to that of some of my other indicators, such as commodities or unemployment. For proof, let's compare the market forecasting record of commod-

TWO SO-SO INDICATORS

Change in T-Bill Rates	Average S&P 400 Gains
Greater than 50%	6.6%
30 to 50	1.2
15 to 30	7.1
10 to 15	0.4
5 to 10	4.8
0 to 5	7.2
−5 to 0	6.8
−10 to −5	8.7
−20 to −10	18.4
−40 to −20	18.2
less than −40	29.5

Twelve-month rate of change in three-month Treasury bill rates as a forecaster of S&P 400 future twelve-month performance.

AAA Corporate Bond Yields	Average S&P 400 Gains
Greater than 20%	2.3%
12.5 to 20	10.8
7.5 to 12.5	8.6
0 to 7.5	5.0
−5 to 0	11.0
−10 to −5	10.0
less than −10	24.7

Twelve-month rate of change in twenty-year AAA corporate bond yields as a forecaster of S&P 400 future twelve-month performance.

ity prices—the rawest expression of inflation—with that of interest rates. As I proved in Chapter 3, the greater the drop in commodity prices, the bigger the boost in stocks. And the greater the rise in commodity prices, the bigger the drop in stocks. This is a very straightforward relationship.

But nothing this firm exists between interest rates and stocks. Again, look at the table. In the past, when short-term interest rates have risen more than 50 percent in a twelve-month period, for example, stocks have not dropped, as you might expect. They have actually risen 6.6 percent on average. And, on average, no matter how much long-term interest rates have risen, stocks have managed to post gains on average.

In one striking example, during the eleven months between August 1973 and July 1974 stocks fell by about 25 percent. True to form, commodity prices during that period were in a dramatic uptrend, rising in nonstop fashion by over 20 percent. In stunning contrast, short-term interest rates actually fell by over 150 basis points. During that period, had short-term rates been your trigger for buying stocks, you probably wouldn't have been able to pay for this book. Had you been following commodity prices, you probably wouldn't have needed this book.

THE MONKEY AND THE ORGAN GRINDER

My bottom line: Interest rates on their own have little or no influence on stock prices. The key is the trend in inflation, which causes both interest rates and stock prices to move. Rates are simply another way to gauge inflation's effect on sustainable economic growth.

To describe the relationship between interest rates and inflation, I always go back to the analogy of the monkey and the organ grinder. Everybody in the crowd watches the monkey because he's more interesting. But it's the organ grinder who's calling the shots.

When it comes to stocks, everybody watches interest rates. But it's the prevailing trend in inflation that really determines the next trend for stocks, and to a large degree where interest rates are headed. In fact, interest rates are an effective gauge of stock market swings only when they reflect the prevailing trend in inflation.

So why do investors set such great store in interest rates as prime movers of stocks? The best way to account for this wrong-headed thinking is to compare it to other myths. Let's consider the common theory among doctors in the 1950s and 1960s that meat eating contributed to good health and longevity.

In the 1990s, thousands of heart attacks later, most people realize just how mistaken this notion of meat eating was. But back then, it seemed eminently plausible.

Where did the docs go wrong? They saw that people who ate more meat tended to live longer, and concluded that meat was responsible for good health. They completely ignored one important fact: Beef is

---

PRIMER ON INTEREST RATES

Interest rates are best gauged through yields on various types of debt, usually bonds. Yield is the annual interest paid out, divided by the price of the bond.

When interest rates rise, bond prices fall because investors aren't willing to pay as much for a bond that will pay them less than current interest rates. When bond prices fall, bond yields rise.

The same process works in reverse when interest rates fall. Then, investors are willing to pay more to get existing bonds' higher rates; bond prices rise and bond yields fall.

As their name indicates, "long-term" interest rates are paid on debt that will be repaid in ten years or more. The best indicator of long-term rates is the yield on bonds issued by America's most creditworthy corporations (rated AAA by the major credit rating services). These bonds typically come due in twenty to thirty years. On such bonds, there's very little risk of default. So changes in AAA bond yields reflect only interest rate swings.

Short-term interest rates are paid on debt that matures in less than a year. The best gauge here is the yield on the shortest-term debt of the U.S. government—Treasury bills. T-bills mature in less than three months and have no default risk. So, fluctuations in T-bill yields reflect only changes in short-term interest rates.

---

expensive. So, people who ate the most beef also tended to be wealthier and could afford the things that tend to prolong life—good housing, hygiene, health care, etc.

A certain amount of wealth, not meat eating, was the key to good health. But because doctors focused solely on the correlation between meat eating and health, they naturally concluded that meat-eating prolonged life.

Similarly, many of those who follow interest rates exclusively have been successful stock investors over the years. That's because interest rates tend to fall when inflation is low, and lower inflation leads to higher stock prices.

But just like the medical researchers of yesteryear, interest-rate groupies are missing the point completely. They can forecast the market correctly most of the time, simply because interest rates usually do drop when inflation is at bay.

But meat eating really doesn't cause good health, any more than interest rates on their own affect stock prices. That's why your returns in the stock market won't be as high if you use interest rates rather than inflation as your basic guide.

I repeat: Falling or rising interest rates do not cause stocks to rise or fall. They simply rise or fall at the same time stocks do most of the time, because of trends in inflation.

RISING RATES CAN BE BULLISH

If inflation is rising along with interest rates, stocks will fall. But if inflation isn't a problem and rates rise, the stock market usually fares well. That's because, in this case, interest rates are rising because the economy is growing and there's more demand for money.

The most convincing proof of this is the great bull market of 1948 to 1965. During that time, stocks rose a massive 500 percent, and generated average annual returns of over 16 percent, including dividends. But short-term interest rates also rose from about 1 percent to over 4 percent. The reason for stocks' climb: Inflation averaged a very tame 1.7 percent.

Higher interest rates during this economic boom reflected faster economic growth that was eminently sustainable. They did not reflect rising inflation, which would have meant the end of economic growth and the bull market.

Bear in mind, inflation can keep on rising, despite efforts to tame it with interest rates. For example, in 1978 and 1980, inflation continued rising sharply in the face of rising interest rates, as commodity prices kept rising.

There's another problem with interest-rate-based investment strategies: Everyone and his brother are constantly on the lookout for interest rate swings.

Anticipating faster growth ahead, investors typically buy stocks when they think the Federal Reserve, the nation's central bank, will step on the economic gas, i.e., lower interest rates. Conversely, anticipating slower growth, they sell stocks when they believe the Fed will slam on the economic brakes, i.e., raise rates.

The Federal Reserve controls rates in three major ways. First, it can raise or lower the discount rate—what it charges banks that belong to the Federal Reserve system when they borrow from it. Second, it can influence the federal funds rate—what banks charge each other for overnight loans. And finally, it can buy or sell Treasury bills—the short-term debt of the U.S. government. When it wants rates to fall, the Fed buys T-bills, thereby pumping more money into the economy. The more money floating around, the less it costs to borrow. When the Fed wants rates to rise, it sells Treasury bills.

The Fed has much more control over short-term interest rates than over long-term ones. The latter are determined largely by the financial markets' outlook for inflation. If the markets expect rising inflation, long-term interest rates edge higher and vice versa. So, the Fed can influence long-term rates only by using short-term rates to control the trend for inflation.

With everybody ready to jump in and out of the market every time the Fed raises an eyebrow, it's not uncommon for the market to head up or down fifty points or more in response to slight shifts, or even the hint of a shift in the Fed's interest rate policy. Consequently, by the time anything does happen, it's almost always too late to buy or sell.

BRAKING TRAIN

Interest rates can be very useful indicators only if they're viewed in the context of inflation. In that case, they accurately reflect trends in economic growth and stocks.

The trend in rates is always affected by what's going on with the economy and inflation. Essentially, the Federal Reserve tries to strike a balance between fighting inflation and promoting economic growth.

To better understand this concept, think about the economy as a train again. Interest rates are essentially the speed pedals of the train. When the train is speeding along too fast, inflation is often the result. In that case, the Federal Reserve hits the brakes by raising interest rates. Because of the threat of inflation, stock prices usually fall.

When rates rise, everyone tends to borrow less; economic growth slows down, and inflation is eventually brought under control. When inflation is not a threat, the Fed usually lets interest rates drop to stimulate economic growth. When rates fall, businesses, consumers, and the government can afford to borrow more. So they spend more. All else being equal, economic growth speeds up. Stock prices rise because growth without inflation looms ahead.

As far as the economy is concerned, the most important thing about interest rates is not whether they're at 8 percent or 12 percent. It's whether they're rising or falling. How hard or softly the Fed steps on the pedals—i.e., how high or low it lets interest rates go—depends to a large degree on the inflation rate.

THE "REAL" INTEREST RATE

My most important interest rate indicator is "real" interest rates, or rates adjusted for inflation. For example, if a bond yields 9 percent and inflation is running at 3 percent, the real interest rate on the bond is 6 percent.

To calculate real rates, you need two pieces of information. First, a measure of inflation. As I've shown, the best long-term indicator of inflation is the twelve-month rate of change in the All Commodity Producer Price Index discussed in Chapter 1.

Second, you need a proxy for long-term interest rates. The current yield of twenty-year AAA corporates (see box, "Primer on Interest Rates," on page 44) will do nicely. A figure for a basket of top-rated bonds is published monthly in *Moody's Bond Record* and *Standard and Poor's Bond Guide*. But all equally rated bonds with the same due dates have roughly the same yield. So any twenty-year AAA bond will do.

As I've said, long-term interest rates are far more closely related to inflation than are short-term rates, like Treasury bill yields. AAA corporates mature (pay off) only after many years. So inflation can erode their value over time. Consequently, AAA corporates' yields are more affected by the inflation rate than are T-bills. Like T-bills, AAA corporates are traded on the open market. So their price reflects market expectations about inflation.

To find what real yields are, subtract the All Commodity PPI's rate of change from the yield on AAA corporate bonds. The difference is inflation-adjusted interest rates, or "real" rates. For example, if AAA corporates are yielding 9 percent and the All Commodity PPI has risen 3 percent in the last twelve months, the "real" interest rate is 6 percent.

Why are real rates such good indicators? Mainly because they reflect future growth expectations. Think about it. When real rates are high, what does it mean? It means corporations are willing to pay interest rates much higher than inflation. That would make sense only if a lot of future real earnings growth is in the cards.

Now look at it from the point of view of those buying the bonds. When growth expectations are high, purchasers of bonds are going to demand higher real rates because there will be alternative investments that will also generate high real rates of return. From either the buyers' or sellers' point of view, high real rates are a reflection of high real growth expectations. And real, i.e., noninflationary, growth almost automatically translates into higher stock prices.

Another key relationship is intertwined. Recall in Chapter 1 that one of the best stock market indicators is the difference between CPI and the All Commodity PPI. When that difference is positive and high, corporate profit margins are high, and stocks tend to rise. When that difference is negative, stocks tend to fall. The reasoning is that the CPI/ACPPI difference relates directly to corporate profit margins. And corporate profit margins are, after all, very strongly related to real growth.

The CPI, not the All Commodity PPI, is most important in determining long-term bond yields. (This means that statistically the correlation between the long-term CPI and bond yields is much higher than the correlation between the long-term All Commodity PPI and bond yields.)

In this sense long-term bond yields are almost a proxy for the CPI. Thus when you subtract the All Commodity PPI from bond yields you are obviously getting a statistic or variable that very closely relates to the difference between CPI and All Commodity PPI, and hence a statistic that will also closely relate to corporate profit margins and hence future real growth.

LESSONS OF HISTORY

How can you tell if real interest rates are high or low? The best way, I've found, is to judge them against their historical average: about 3.6 percentage points. In other words, AAA corporate bond yields have averaged about 3.6 percentage points above the current rate of inflation.

Whenever real rates have been higher than their historical average, the economy is poised for strong growth. In such times, inflation has been less of a threat, so potential for sustained economic growth is greater than ever. A bull market in stocks is normally raging at such times.

As you can see from the chart below, the relationship between real rates and stocks is far more consistent than the relationship between stocks and both short-term and long-term interest rates. Specifically, the higher real rates are, the better stocks have performed.

For example, since 1954, whenever real rates have been more than 12 percentage points, stocks have tacked on average annual gains of 34.7 percent. The last time that happened was back in May 1986. Stocks were then on their way to a 50 percent gain in the next fifteen months.

On the other hand, low real interest rates have generally presaged market declines. Under such conditions, real economic growth is low,

REAL RATES AND STOCKS

Real Rates	S&P 400 12 Months Later
Greater than 12	+34.7%
10 to 12	+17.5
9 to 10	+17.0
5 to 9	+5.8
3 to 5	+8.7
0 to 3	+6.7
−5 to 0	+7.0
less than −5	−1.1

Level of real interest rates as a forecaster for S&P 400 future twelve-month performance.

prospects for corporate profits are dim, and inflation—not sustainable economic growth—is driving the economy. The market is headed for a fall.

As the table shows, lower real interest rates are directly related to lower stock market returns. The extreme is negative real rates in which interest rates are actually lower than the rate of inflation. This happens only when inflation is raging, a prescription for stock market meltdowns.

The average return for stocks under such conditions is −1.1 percent. But losses can be much worse. For example, in October 1973, AAA corporate bonds were yielding 10 percent below the inflation rate. Stocks plummeted more than 40 percent over the next twelve months.

ONE SIMPLE RULE

As I've shown, the higher real rates go, the better. Unfortunately, they rarely reach 12 percent or higher, the point where you're practically guaranteed huge windfall profits. But you can generally count on a bull market to continue as long as real rates stay above 1 percentage point.

My trading rule is this: Buy stocks when real rates are at least 2 percentage points and sell when they go below 1 percentage point.

Look at the table "My Trading Rule." Since 1949, this strategy has never failed to produce big profits. Sure, you might have had to ride out a downturn or two. But as our table shows, in every period when these conditions have held, investors have wound up with sizable gains.

Another advantage is that your total number of trades would have been very low. In fact, since 1949, you would have had just five sell signals. The last buy signal was in April 1981, and it's still in effect as of early 1993. During that time, there have been several selloffs and bear markets. But stocks have tripled in value. In fact, there has been literally no better long-term trading rule for investors who want to buy stocks and lock them away.

MY TRADING RULE

Period Holding Stocks	Gain by S&P 400
Feb 52 to May 56	24.05 to 49.64
Nov 57 to Apr 66	43.41 to 98.17
July 66 to Feb 73	91.95 to 127.90
Oct 75 to June 77	99.29 to 109.50
Aug 77 to Aug 78	107.50 to 115.0
April 81 to Present	152.30 to 463

Results of trading strategy of buying stocks when real interest rates rise above 2 percent, and selling when real rates fall below 1 percent.

THE LONG AND SHORT OF IT

There's another related interest rate indicator that I find just as useful as real interest rates: the ratio of AAA bond yields to Treasury bill yields.

Again, this ratio tries to get at the relationships among interest rates, real growth, and inflation. The key is this: Inflation affects long-term interest rates much more strongly than it does short-term rates. Historically, the wider the difference between the two rates, the better stocks have performed.

Again, the best proxy for short-term rates is Treasury bills; the best proxy for long-term rates is AAA-rated corporate bonds maturing in twenty years or more.

To figure my ratio, simply find the current yield on twenty-year AAA bonds and divide by the current rate paid by ninety-day Treasury bills. For example, if AAA bonds are yielding 9 percent and T-bills are yielding 5 percent, the ratio is 1.80 to 1.

My rule: Buy stocks when the ratio is above 1.20, and sell when it dips below 1.10. This strategy would have netted you an average annual gain of 12.8 percent had you started following it in January 1949. The table on page 52, "Another Good Trading Rule," shows the other results.

The reason my rule has worked so well is that the Federal Reserve tends to lower short-term rates when the economy is growing slowly

ANOTHER GOOD TRADING RULE

Period Holding Stocks	% Change in S&P 400
Jan 49 to Nov 59 (130)	303.55%
Mar 60 to Dec 65 (69)	66.34
Mar 67 to Dec 68 (21)	21.01
June 70 to Jun 73 (36)	41.27
Oct 74 to Oct 78 (18)	43.87
June 80 to Oct 80 (4)	15.22
Nov 81 to Feb 82 (3)	−6.75
Aug 82 to Jun 89 (82)	202.85
Feb 90 (21)	20.74

Results of trading strategy based on buying stocks when AAA corporate/T-bill ratio was above 1.20, and selling when it fell below 1.10.

or not at all to stimulate growth. Meanwhile, long-term rates tend to remain high due to fear of inflation.

At this point in the cycle, inflation is whipped. Potential for faster economic growth with no inflation is high; stocks can take off to new highs. As the economy begins to revive, bond investors come to believe that inflation is down for the count. Consequently, the gap between short and long-term rates begins to narrow. Stocks' potential gains shrink.

Finally, the gap between short- and long-term interest rates narrows to the point where our ratio falls below 1.1. At that point, economic growth has probably peaked and inflation begins to be a threat. Stocks plummet.

Why is it curtains for stocks when short-term rates edge up on long-term rates? Once again, it goes back to the question of whether or not economic growth is sustainable. Long-term interest rates, as I said above, essentially represent businesses' demand for long-term loans, which they use to finance expansion—i.e., to build plants, hire workers, enlarge distribution lines, etc.

Businesses usually borrow with as big a payback period as possible to make sure that their investments have enough time to turn profitable. Usually, short-term loans just don't make it. Businesses borrow long term at high rates only if they expect to grow considerably between now and when the loans are due. The more growth businesses are expecting, the higher long-term rates will be. So long-term rates reflect expectations of growth: real growth plus inflation.

Short-term interest rates, however, are driven by expectations for inflation between now and when the loan is due. If long-term interest rates are much higher than short-term ones, it means that companies expect their earnings to grow considerably, after inflation is taken into account. So it's also a sign that stocks are the place to be.

The ratio of AAA-bond yields to Treasury bill yields doesn't have a perfect record. For example, when deflation is in force, the ratio can be in positive territory even while stocks plummet. That's what happened during the Great Depression.

But this ratio is about as close to perfection as any interest rate indicator around. Following it alone will put money in your pocket most of the time.

DOESN'T RATE

The two inflation-based interest rate indicators described above— real interest rates and the AAA-bond/T-bill yield ratio—are the best for using interest rates to trade stocks. You can beat the market by following either or both of them.

But keep in mind that even though they both take inflation into account, their record in forecasting stock prices is not as good as the record for commodity prices (see Chapter 2).

Although interest rates are an important piece of the economic puzzle, they fall last among the other basic building blocks of my overall strategy: inflation, unemployment, money supply, and price-to-earnings ratios. And remember, interest rates are only effective in forecasting stocks to the degree that they reflect the trend in inflation.

The key variable affecting stocks is inflation, not interest rates. And following interest rates exclusively can present a misleading picture of stocks' future. Stocks may buck up or down in response to interest rate swings in the short term, as traders attempt to jockey for advantage. But don't make the mistake of believing that an interest rate swing always precedes an equal and opposite reaction in stocks.

Most of the time, changes in rates correspond to changes in inflation. But not always. And only if they do correspond will stocks rise or fall. I can't stress this enough: Interest rates do not affect stocks on their own.

So good as the rules I've laid down in this chapter are, you'll still do far better if you use them in conjunction with the other indicators in this book. Following interest rates as an exclusive gauge for trading stocks just doesn't work.

POINTS TO REMEMBER

1. Interest rates are poor predictors of stock market trends, unless they're put into the context of inflation—as "real" interest rates.
2. "Real," or inflation-adjusted, interest rates are best expressed as the yield on twenty-year AAA-rated corporate bonds minus the twelve-month rate of change in the All Commodity Producer Price Index. The higher real rates are, the more bullish for stocks.
3. The higher the difference between long- (twenty-year AAA bond yields) and short-term interest rates (three-month Treasury bill yields), the more bullish for stocks.

5

Money Supply:
Go with the Flow

"MONEY MAKES THE WORLD GO ROUND." "It takes money to make money." "Money is the root of all evil." "Time is money."

Outside of love, it's hard to find anything about which so many clichés are said daily. They're a testament to just how important money is.

But despite all the attention money gets, very few people realize its true impact on the economy. And I'm not just talking about small investors. Many Wall Street veterans I know have only a hazy notion of how the supply of greenbacks affects stocks.

The fact is, there are certain levels of growth in the money supply that go hand in hand with a rising stock market. If money growth goes much below or beyond these marks, both the economy and stocks tend to tank.

I'm not saying that watching the money supply will always get you in and out of stocks at all the right times. But it will help you rule out the two biggest stock market killers: inflation and deflation. Because of this, money supply is very important to watch.

WATERING HOLE

Like the Nile in ancient Egypt, money is the source of our economic life. If more of it is flowing through, it's easier for businesses and consumers to get loans. As this cash is spent, the economy becomes greener, more vibrant.

Just as the Nile region fared best when water was flowing at a steady rate, our economy (and stock market) is healthiest when the supply of money is rising slowly and steadily.

If money growth is too sluggish—or worse, falling—economic activity dries up. Businesses find it hard to borrow so they usually lay off workers; consumers don't have as much to spend. You can then count on a recession and a plunge in stocks until the money flow increases.

There's no more striking example of what a drought of money can do than the Great Depression. Between October 1929 and April 1933, the money supply fell by an incredible 33 percent!

The results were catastrophic. During those three and a half years, unemployment climbed to over 25 percent, and average household income was cut nearly in half. The stock market, an unmitigated horror, lost over 75 percent of its value.

But too-fast money growth is also bad news for stocks, just as a flood can be as destructive as a drought. Whenever there's too much money floating around, its value decreases; you can't buy as much as you used to with the same amount of cash. The result is rising inflation, which causes financial assets like stocks and bonds to tank.

So, having just the right amount of growth in the money supply—not too much, not too little—is crucial for a healthy stock market. Otherwise, deflation or inflation rears its ugly head and wreaks havoc.

DAMMING THE FLOW

Controlling the flow of money is the job of the Federal Reserve, this country's central bank. It tries to prevent monetary floods and droughts by lowering or raising certain key short-term interest rates. The Fed's actions affect all other interest rates and act as a giant upstream dam.

As interest rates fall, banks tend to make more loans. When they do, they basically create money that didn't exist before, and this comes pouring into the economy. When interest rates rise, fewer loans are usually made, so the supply of money doesn't grow as fast, and sometimes it even shrinks.

The Fed has a very tough job because there's no one optimal rate of money supply growth; that depends on what's going on in the economy.

Moreover, when the Fed lowers interest rates, the supply of money doesn't always expand. Between mid-1990 and mid-1991, for example, the Fed lowered short-term interest rates from 8 percent to 5.8 percent. Yet the money supply didn't grow any faster; it actually shrank. And there were many times, especially in the seventies, when interest rates rose but money growth did too.

The problem is that growth in the money supply does not depend solely on interest rates, just like your weight doesn't depend only on how much you eat. Other things, like banks' willingness to make loans, also affect money supply. So after the Fed lowers interest rates, it takes weeks before the impact on the money supply is known.

Because it can't predict the future, the Fed tends to overreact. From February to October 1987, for example, annual money supply growth was cut nearly in half (from about 10 percent to 5 percent). That dip was one of the sharpest on record and was a major contributor to the crash of 1987, when stocks fell by over 30 percent in just two weeks.

Another big monetary squeeze came between January and September 1973. Back then, annual growth in the money supply dropped from 12.7 percent to just 7.4 percent. This set the stage for the bruiser recession of 1973–75, and the calamitous 1974 bear market, in which many stocks lost half their value or more.

Conversely, the Fed sometimes lowers interest rates too much and causes a monetary flood. This is especially true when the country is coming out of a recession and the central bank doesn't want to risk another economic downturn.

But remember: A flood of money can be just as bad as a drought. When too many greenbacks are floating around, there's often a burst of inflation. Between mid-1974 and early 1975, for example, the Fed cut short-term interest rates by more than half (from nearly 13 percent to about 5 percent). Growth in the money supply soared from under 6 percent to nearly 10 percent by mid-1975.

Not surprisingly, the economy snapped out of the recession with a bang and stocks staged one of their greatest rallies. Unfortunately, the Fed kept interest rates too low, too long; the money supply continued to grow more than 10 percent annually for three whole years. It's no wonder that inflation started spiraling in the late 1970s and early 1980s.

OTHER THEORIES

The Fed can't be blamed for its excesses because controlling the money supply is an inexact procedure. But this hasn't stopped people from trying to make the whole process more automatic.

Some folks, for example, still think we should be on the gold standard, which was abandoned in the 1970s. For every dollar, they want to see an equivalent amount of gold in the government's coffers to make good on the paper money. But the gold standard was done away with for good reason. It doesn't work well when economic events unfold rapidly, as in the late 1920s and early 1930s, and the late 1960s and early 1970s. In fact, the gold standard is widely considered to have helped foster the Great Depression.

A more mainstream view about the "right" amount of money is monetarism, popularized in the late 1970s by Milton Friedman. Monetarists firmly believe that the amount of money floating around determines the inflation rate. So they think the money supply should grow only as fast as the economy can expand without triggering rising inflation.

This theory works only under certain circumstances. Former Fed Chairman Paul Volcker put it to a test in the early 1980s by drastically cutting money supply growth by 7 percentage points. Although inflation did ultimately fall, there was no proof that the Fed's clampdown was the cause.

Moreover, in early 1983 the Fed pumped up money supply growth to a torrid 13 percent annual rate to revive the economy. In the past, similar moves had set off inflation. This time, inflation remained in check because the down-and-out economy had a great deal of room to rebound.

FED-WATCHERS CLUB

So, none of these cut-and-dry approaches to money supply growth have worked. Instead, the Fed continues to do the best it can, given the latest economic data. And Wall Street analysts and traders watch the Fed's moves like hawks. The financial media have also picked up on Fed watching in a big way.

CNBC, a cable TV station, reports daily whether the Fed has eased credit, tightened credit, or done nothing to influence short-term interest rates, which presumably affect the money supply.

Depending on the Fed's actions, the stock market sometimes swings sharply up or down. But don't pay attention to such swings; they very seldom signal important changes. That's because shifts in money supply can be gauged only over longer periods of time. This means you have plenty of time to act.

MONEY INDICATORS

To find out whether money supply trends will help or hurt stocks, I've developed three basic indicators: my Rule of Three, Delta-M, and monthly changes in M2. They're based on seventy years of statistics, and when it comes to forecasting money trends they've almost never missed a call.

All three indicators are based on a simple relationship: I compare the current trend in money supply growth with past levels that have typically supported long-term rallies in stocks.

First, let me explain briefly how money is measured. Just as people who work on a river use various yardsticks to gauge a river's flow, economists use several measurements to calculate money supply. The two most common are called M1 and M2.

M1 includes all cash in circulation (like the money in your wallet), as well as the money in your checking account. M2 includes savings accounts and money market funds, in addition to what is in M1. Two other measures, M3 and L, include all of M2 plus such obscure items as repurchase agreements and overnight transfers of $1 million or more between banks.

In general the Ms tend to mirror one another, but there are some subtle, important differences. M2 is more inclusive than M1. Though its components are spendable, some are less likely to be spent than are the components of M1. For example, savings accounts are more likely to be socked away for longer periods of time than are any of the components of M1. This means that M1 is likely to find its way into the economic river faster than M2.

What I have found is that gauging changes in M1 is the best way to predict inflation. M2 is a little more important when it comes to predicting real growth. Thus, when I predict changes in the stock market, M1 is a bit more important. But when it comes to predicting economic growth (see Chapter 13), M2 is more important.

In almost all cases, however, you can substitute one for the other, without much loss in predictive power. Because the most reliable historical information is available for M2, we've used it in our models below. What's called M2 today is very similar to what Milton Friedman and Anna Schwartz called M3 in their classic work, *A Monetary History of the United States, 1867–1960*. It is the best source of historical data on the money supply.

The indicators that follow are based on M2. But they would only have to be varied slightly to work for M1. Moreover, M1 actually works better than M2 when it comes to combining money supply with other variables for an overall model of the market. But again the differences are small and, in general, what you say about one holds for the other.

Fortunately, finding money supply figures is a relatively simple matter. Each week the Federal Reserve compiles more money supply data in its "Money Stock" Statistical Release than you'll ever possibly need. Each report lists twenty-four months of data on all the various M–money supply measures, including up-to-date figures for the most recent period. Figures for the previous month are released in about the middle of every month. It's available for a few bucks by calling the Federal Reserve Publications Office (202-452-3245). For historical data, call the Fed's Freedom of Information Department at 202-452-3684. You can also get these data from the Department of

Commerce bulletin board or from a service like Telerate or Data Resources, Inc.

Although the Federal Reserve Statistical Release is probably the best source, recent M2 figures also appear in most local papers' financial sections, as well as in *The Wall Street Journal* and *Barron's*. Copies of these can be found on microfiche at most libraries. Note that though revisions to the Ms have been minor in recent years, it's a good idea to check each week to make sure that the previous months' data have not been revised. Figures also appear in the *Survey of Current Business*, page C-4, series 106. Use seasonally adjusted figures.

DEPRESSION GAUGE

My first indicator, the Rule of Three, basically tells you when the money supply is shrinking, i.e., when the river is drying up. If it is, it may be time to bail out of stocks in a big way—depression and a catastrophic drop in stocks could be on the horizon. Let's see how it works.

First, we find monthly M2 and M1 money supply figures for each of the past eight months from the Federal Reserve Statistical Release. For example, if it's July 1993, we find figures for each month from November 1992 through June 1993.

Next we add up the monthly M2 money supply figures for April, May, and June—the most recent three-month period—and divide by three to get an average. We do the same thing for January, February, and March, the three-month period immediately before the most recent one. If the April through June average is less than the January through March average, the money supply is shrinking. The Rule of Three is flashing red this month. The first part of the rule is negative.

To see if the second part of the signal is also red, we compare the average monthly money supply from March through May 1993 with that of December 1992 through February 1993. If the March through May period had an average M2 of $2.1 trillion and December through February period had one of $2.2 trillion, for example, we could again say the money supply was shrinking. The second part of the Rule of Three would also be flashing red.

Finally, we compare the last three-month period, from February through April, with that of November 1992 though January 1993. If the average M2 of February through April is less than that of November through January, the third part of the Rule of Three is also negative. We then perform the same calculation for M1. If it's also been negative three months running, a red signal is triggered.

Once a red signal is triggered, a green will occur only when the most recent three months have a higher average M2 than the previous three months, for three months in a row. For example, the average M2 from May through July (the latest three-month period) would have to be greater than the average M2 from February through April, the previous three-month period. Similarly, the average M2 from June through August would have to be greater than that from March through May. And finally, the average of July through September would have to be higher than the average M2 from April through June. The same must also be true of M1.

DEPRESSION GAUGE

A warning from the Rule of Three doesn't guarantee a major recession or depression. But this critical signpost doesn't often speak. When it does, history has shown that stocks are a disaster waiting to happen.

From 1922 to 1949, the Rule of Three gave a red light five times. (See "Rule of Three.") Had you sold each of those times, and bought back stocks when the rule flashed a green light, you would have rolled up a compounded gain (excluding dividends) of 1,860 percent!

You would have been high and dry during the great crash of October 1929, and back in the market months later to pick up the bargains that followed. In contrast, a simple buy-and-hold strategy during those volatile twenty-eight years would not have even doubled your money (excluding dividends)!

Look at the two sell signals in May 1929 and February 1930. What they suggest is that the Great Depression didn't begin with the Crash of 1929. Rather it started when the money supply started shrinking in 1930.

Indeed, had the Fed tried to increase the money supply in 1930, the 1929 crash would probably have been remembered much like the 1962 and 1987 crashes—as just a correction in a long-term bull market.

THE RULE OF THREE

Signal Date	Signal	DJIA*	Percentage Change
Feb 1922	Buy	89.05	+ 275%
May 1929	Sell	333.79	+ 28
Oct 1929	Buy	238.95	+ 20
Feb 1930	Sell	286.10	+ 66
Oct 1933	Buy	98.14	+ 41
Sept 1937	Sell	138.17	+ 3
May 1938	Buy	133.88	+ 36
July 1948	Sell	181.71	+ 6
Oct 1948	Buy	171.20	+ 1
Jan 1949	Sell	173.06	− 3
July 1949–Present	Buy	178.66	+ 1754
Compounded Gain			+36,261%

* Return from buying stocks each time when Rule of Three is positive, and selling when it is negative.

GROWTH IS GOOD

Since 1949, the money supply has been growing constantly. So our Rule of Three has been continuously flashing green. True to form, it's been an exceptional period for stocks, an average annual gain of 12.2 percent.

In fact, stocks have outperformed every other investment group over that time: bonds, cash, real estate, and metals. They've had their ups and downs. But over the long run, they've been the place to be.

Although you can rule out deflation and depression when the Rule of Three is flashing green, you can't rule out anything else that may harm the stock market, such as inflation or recession. During the bear markets of 1974 and 1987, for example, The Rule of Three was lit up in green.

So the best way to use the Rule of Three is as a long-term gauge for getting out of the market. When it flashes red, a stock-crushing depression may be on the way. That's the time to get worried. Otherwise, the money supply flow should remain high enough to keep the economy going, and stocks will be subject to relatively short bear markets. This is good news if you're saving for retirement.

RECESSION ALERT

The Rule of Three is small comfort when it comes to forecasting short-term drops in stocks, like the crash of 1987. These are often caused by cuts in the money supply's rate of growth, rather than its absolute shrinkage.

To forecast such twists and turns, I use an indicator called Delta-M. This measures the change in the growth rate of M2. Delta-M is simply the average monthly change in M2 over the last six months, divided by the average monthly change for the twelve months before that.

Delta-M is an excellent bear market gauge. And it's no wonder. A sharply negative Delta-M means a sharp contraction in money growth. The Fed is damming up the money river's flow, so drought lies ahead for the economy and the stock market.

A sharply negative Delta-M is not as extreme a signal as the flashing red of our Rule of Three. But it does mean you should bail out of stocks and buy back later at a cheaper price.

Look at the table. Whenever Delta-M has been less than −.30, for example, stock market gains have been almost nil. And when Delta-M has punctured below −.40, the average stock has lost a staggering 17 percent over the next twelve months.

In August 1987, for instance, Delta-M hit −.63. This was a sure tip-off that problems lay ahead for stocks, just as the Rule of Three told us that eventually things would come out all right.

There's no disputing that Delta-M can be counted on to get you out of stocks at the right time. Its usefulness as a buy signal, however, is limited. Generally, the more Delta-M is increasing, the faster M-2 growth is growing, and the more the stock market is likely to gain. However, as you can see from the table "Delta-M and the S&P 400," the average gains vary wildly.

When Delta-M has been in the .30 to .40 range, for example, stocks have averaged 16.9 percent gains over the next twelve months. But when Delta-M has been between .40 and .60, the gain has been only

DELTA-M AND THE S&P 400

Delta-M	S&P 400 12 Months Later
Greater than .60	14.4%
.40 to .60	5.2
.30 to .40	16.9
.20 to .30	11.9
.10 to .11	10.5
0 to .10	8.8
−.10 to 0	9.4
−.20 to −.10	11.1
−.30 to −.20	9.3
−.40 to −.30	4.1
Less than −.40	−17.0

Level of Delta-M as a forecaster for S&P 400 future twelve-month performance.

5.2 percent! Moreover, when Delta-M has been over .60, the average gain moves back up to 14.4 percent.

Finally, note that while Delta-M is not particularly useful as a buying tool, it can help pinpoint economic recoveries. In fact, Delta-M has turned positive just as each postwar recession was ending. A positive Delta-M is, therefore, necessary (but not enough evidence)

SECOND INDICATOR: CALCULATING RATE OF CHANGE IN M2 (DELTA-M)

1. Get monthly figures for M2 for the past 18 months.
2. Figure out the average monthly rate of change for each of the 18 months. If in June 1992, for example, M2 is $3331 billion, while in May 1992 it's $3327.6 billion, that's a 0.10 percent increase.
3. Now average the rates for the first 12 months.
4. Average the rates for the last 6 months.
5. To find Delta-M, take the average rate of change for the most recent six months and subtract the average rate of change for the preceding 12 months. That's all there is to it. When Delta-M is negative, it means that money growth in the most recent six months is less than in the previous 12 months. That's a sell signal for stocks. See the table "Delta-M and the S&P 400" to see how stocks have performed at different levels of Delta-M.

THIRD INDICATOR: MONTHLY CHANGE IN M2

Here's how to track changes in monthly M2 growth:

1. Obtain data for the most recent two months on the size of M2, for example, May and June.
2. Divide the most recent month's figure by the previous one. For example, divide June's by May's. Subtract 1 from the result to find the month-to-month percentage gain. For example, if May's figure is $4.15 billion and June's is $4.16 billion, the monthly rate of increase is 0.24 percent.
3. Compare the result from step 2 with the results on the table that shows monthly changes in M2 and average corresponding 12-month gains in stocks. That's all there is to it.

---

for the beginning of an economic recovery. The box entitled "Second Indicator: Calculating Rate of Change in M2 (Delta-M)" has specific instructions on how to calculate Delta-M.

INFLATION AND DEFLATION PROOFING

Inflation, of course, is the other danger that threatens stocks. If it's out of control, there's simply no way the market can thrive. And runaway inflation can bring on a recession. That's because the Fed is likely to raise interest rates and starve the economy for money. If the rate of money supply growth is slow and steady, however, there's almost no chance inflation will rage.

Just what constitutes slow and steady has changed over time, due to shifts in employment, producer prices, and other factors. Still, there's a range of money growth that's proven optimal.

And this brings me to my third indicator: twelve-month M2 growth. Look at the table "M2 and the S&P 400." Whenever M2 growth has averaged between 0.2 and 0.5 percent a month for a year, stocks have almost always done well over the next twelve months.

In other words, if you buy stocks when money growth is in that

M2 AND THE S&P 400

M2 Growth	S&P 400
1.00 or More	−0.2
.90 to 1.00	0.1
.80 to .90	−0.5
.50 to .80	7.9
.40 to .50	13.1
.30 to .40	16.5
.20 to .30	20.2
Less Than .20	0.7

Monthly M2 growth as a forecaster of S&P 400 future 12-month performance.

range, you won't have to worry about inflation or deflation. And you'll most likely score big gains during the next twelve months.

Since the end of World War II, whenever the money supply has grown between 0.2 percent and 0.3 percent from month to month, stocks have gained an average of 20.2 percent over the next 12 months. This rate of money growth is moderate and most bullish for stocks.

If the monthly growth in M2 is 0.24 percent, for example, we've hit the most bullish reading on the chart. It's time to buy stocks! You can expect a 20.2 percent gain in equities over the next twelve months. The biggest gains were in 1954 when the market soared over 40 percent in the twelve months following moderate money growth.

Only in 1957–58 and 1989–90 did the stock market lose ground during periods of moderately slow money growth. In 1990, the culprit was the Persian Gulf crisis. In 1957–58, the Fed overdid it. Then, moderate money growth quickly turned too slow and a mini–bear market followed.

What's too slow for money growth? Anything less than 0.2 percent each month. In such cases, the stock market has risen only 0.7 percent over the next twelve months. Cash would be a far better place to be.

What's too fast for money growth? Anything more than 1 percent each month. In such cases, stocks have lost an average of 0.17 percent over the next twelve months. Again, you'd be far better off holding cash. For details on how to calculate average monthly changes in M2, see the box entitled "Third Indicator: Monthly Change in M2."

MONEY ISN'T EVERYTHING

As I mentioned earlier, my three money indicators are best used as bear market signals. Here's a wrap-up of how you should react to them as a group:

1. When my Rule of Three is flashing red, get out of stocks. A major recession or depression is on the way.

2. When Delta-M is very negative, i.e., less than −.30, a sharp economic downturn is on the horizon. Although you can try to weather the storm, my advice is to get out of the market and enter again when all's clear.

3. When the average monthly change in money supply is more than 1 percent or less than 0.20 percent, be very cautious about new investment in stocks; either the economy is growing too fast or we're on the verge of a recession.

Following my three money indicators—and no others—would have kept you well ahead of the game for the past sixty or seventy years. Few if any other guideposts have this kind of long-term record.

Still, my three indicators aren't foolproof. In fact, as we've pointed out, they may miss several of the market's short-term flips and twists.

And they're generally ineffective when it comes to pinpointing market tops and bottoms. The most striking example of their ambiguity came in 1956–57. When the stock market hit a bottom in December 1957, for example, Delta-M was −0.79. But at the July 1956 top, Delta-M was practically identical. More recently, at the market top in October 1983, Delta-M hit −.379, but it gave a similar reading during the bottom in July 1984.

My third indicator has similar flaws. The average monthly growth rate in money supply was 0.65 when stocks peaked in February 1980. But it was identical when stocks bottomed during April of that year. Also, the monthly growth rate was 0.40 before stocks bottomed in October 1990, one of the greatest buying opportunities of all time. But it was almost identical in August 1987, before one of the biggest crashes in the stock market's history.

So, steady money supply growth doesn't guarantee a rising stock market, any more than a healthy flow in the Nile ensured a booming economy. The success of the Nile region depended on several additional things, such as soil quality, temperature, and security from invaders. Likewise, money isn't the only thing that the economy and stocks need for good health.

The other core indicators discussed in this book—commodity prices, unemployment insurance claims, interest rates, and price-to-earnings ratios (the subject of our next chapter)—also have a place in an on-target investment strategy.

Tracking money supply growth can't predict these variables. But it can rule out the two most destructive forces that can affect the stock market: hyperinflation and deflation.

So, while money is not everything, understanding how it can hurt or help your stock holdings is a vital key to successful investing. And if you use the indicators in this chapter in conjunction with the others in this book, you'll find that money does indeed talk . . . and loudly.

POINTS TO REMEMBER

1. Money supply growth is the river upon which all economic life depends. The Federal Reserve regulates money supply growth to maintain the optimum flow for promoting sustainable economic growth.
2. The Rule of Three tells you when the money supply flow is shrinking dramatically. At such times, a possible deflationary depression is in store, and stocks are about to get skewered.
3. Delta-M tells you when the rate of change in money growth is slowing down sharply, leading to a slowdown in economic growth. That's a warning sign to exit stocks.
4. Monthly changes in the M2 money supply measure the flow of money into the system at any time. Too rapid growth signals that inflation is a threat to stocks. Too slow growth means that deflation is a threat.

6

P/Es: The Key to Value

PORSCHES ARE GREAT CARS. But I'd never pay a million bucks for one. And I doubt anyone else would, either; not even my friend Fred who nearly mortgaged his house to buy a new Alfa Romeo.

But many people do buy stocks that are as ridiculously overpriced as million-dollar Porsches. That's because few realize that the greatest company in the world can be the absolute worst stock to buy if the price is too high.

I always go back to the case of IBM in late 1961. At that time, Big Blue was truly America's dream growth company. At the forefront of the computer revolution, IBM had seen its earnings grow more than 25 percent a year for more than eight years. And they would continue to rise at that pace into the early 1970s.

Yet, investors who bought the stock in late 1961 got creamed. From its high in 1961 to its low in 1962, IBM stock fell by more than 50 percent. Why? Because it had been bid up to unsustainable heights. It was simply too expensive. The best tip-off: The stock traded at a P/E of 70, or seventy times its earnings per share for the previous twelve months.

Let me explain. In the long run, a company's stock price rises or falls based on how fast its earnings grow. By comparing a stock's price to the earnings of the company, you can see how fast investors expect those profits to grow.

A price-to-earnings ratio, or P/E, is a company's stock price per share divided by the annual earnings per share of the company. P/Es represent how much investors are willing to pay for each dollar of the company's actual earnings per share. For example, if a stock has a P/E of 10, investors are paying $10 for each $1 of profits.

Generally, the more sure investors are of a company's continuing growth and the more they expect that growth to be, the more they'll pay for each dollar of its current earnings per share. In other words, the greater investors' optimism about a company, the higher its stock's P/E will be.

Problems inevitably arise when investors are overly optimistic. IBM's P/E of 70 back in late 1961 indicated that investors were expecting the company to grow several times faster than the typical company for an indefinite period of time.

Even with its fabulous potential back in early 1961, the company couldn't possibly have done that. If it had, we'd be living in the United States of IBM today. Investors' optimism was simply out of touch with reality. And the best warning of that was IBM's unrealistically high P/E.

In other words, IBM stock in late 1961 was the equivalent of a Porsche selling for a million bucks. It was a great company. But it wasn't a good deal. At the slightest hint of disappointment, IBM stock dropped dramatically.

FATHERS OF VALUE INVESTING

P/Es can also tell us when stocks are cheap. In their now legendary book *Principles and Techniques of Security Analysis,* Benjamin Graham and David Dodd proposed that one important key to successful long-term investing is to buy stocks with low P/Es.

A stock with a low P/E, they reasoned, is selling at a price that's cheap relative to its earnings. At some point, they postulated, investors will realize that the company's future prospects were worth more, and they'll bid the stock price up.

The other side of the coin is that stocks selling at relatively high P/Es have been bid up too high relative to their earnings. At some point, investors will realize that they have paid too much for those shares, and they'll either sell or stop buying. Either way, the high P/E stocks would underperform the low P/E stocks.

How can you tell a low P/E stock from a high P/E issue? The best way is by looking at its relative P/E: how its P/E compares with that of the average stock. IBM in 1962, for example, sold at seventy times earnings. But just as important, its P/E was three times that of the average S&P 400 stock.

The Graham-Dodd guidelines can also be applied to the stock market as a whole. In other words, just as an individual stock can sell above or below its realistic growth potential, so can stocks in general. The average we use is the P/E of the S&P 400.

Generally, the lower the P/E of the S&P 400, the greater the chance that stocks will rise. The higher its P/E, the greater the chance that stocks will drop.

Many of the biggest fortunes on Wall Street were built by those smart enough to buy stocks when no one else wanted them. Low P/Es were one of the best tipoffs that the market was a bargain. At such times, stocks are the least vulnerable to bad news. These savvy folks then sold when equities became the rage, when P/Es were relatively high. At such times, stocks are the most vulnerable to bad news. J. P. Morgan, John Paul Getty, John Templeton, and Warren Buffett are but a few of these great contrarians.

HOW HIGH IS TOO HIGH?

The torch that Messrs. Graham and Dodd lit still burns brightly today. In fact, everyone on Wall Street now watches P/Es out of the corner of his or her eye to see if stocks are cheap or dear, except for perhaps hard-core technical analysts.

It's true that compared to other stock price indicators, P/Es do the best job by far of showing when equities are generally cheap or dear (see box "Best Value Indicator").

What P/Es of market averages don't do, at least by themselves, is to tell us reliably when stock prices are too high to mount an advance, or too cheap to fall further. In other words, P/Es don't tell us when stocks have peaked or bottomed. Consequently, they're really not effective at telling us when to buy, hold, or sell stocks.

For all the lip service that's paid to P/Es as an indicator, no one has come up with a reliable rule for using them to time the market. This is

---

BEST VALUE INDICATOR

When it comes to valuing stocks, P/Es are clearly the best indicator around. For proof, compare them with the other two most widely used value indicators: the price-to-book-value ratio and dividend yields.

Like P/Es, the idea behind these value measures is that the lower they are, the cheaper stocks are. But unlike P/Es, there are numerous problems with using them.

A price-to-book-value ratio compares a company's stock price to its total assets per share. Specifically, it's the stock price divided by the company's equity (total assets less total debt) per share.

But asset values can be altered by a thousand accounting tricks. Consequently, book values can be severely over- or understated, and stocks with low price-to-book-value ratios can actually be expensive. Similarly, stocks with high price-to-book-value ratios can be cheap.

Dividend yields are basically what the company pays out to shareholders in annual dividends, as a percentage of the stock price. For example, if a stock costs $10 per share and pays a $1 per share annual dividend, its dividend yield is 10 percent.

Companies can maintain dividends at unsustainably high rates for long periods of time, before they're forced to cut them. And stocks often hit bottom right after dividends are cut. Consequently, dividend yields can also give a misleading signal as to whether stocks are unusually cheap or dear.

Another problem with both dividend yields and price-to-book-value ratios is that they're both static measures. They reflect the past and ignore earnings—the key driving force behind stocks.

The key question for investors is whether stocks are expensive or cheap relative to their prospects for sustainable earnings growth. And in this regard, only P/Es tell the story. Only P/Es compare a company's earnings to its stock price.

---

understandable. The reason is that no one has a truly reliable benchmark for saying when P/Es are relatively high or low.

Sometimes a seemingly very low P/E has been a sign of an impending top in stocks. In November 1980, for example, the market's P/E was barely above 10. Stocks crashed some 25 percent in the next twenty-one months. Other times, a much higher P/E has coincided with a major market rally. In fact, in August 1986 the market's P/E was above 17. In the next year stocks roared ahead by over 40 percent.

Or consider the mid-1970s and early 1980s. From October 1973 through August 1982, the average S&P stock traded at a P/E of just 9.7, but stocks didn't budge. The only gains investors realized were in dividends. Actually the S&P 400 was a bit lower in August 1982 than in October 1973.

In that case, investors were right not to bid up P/Es (and stocks) to high levels. Only in the latter part of the 1980s would low-P/E investors have been rewarded for buying stocks in the mid-1970s.

Or consider the early 1960s, when P/Es were much higher, yet stocks managed to perform much better than in the mid-1970s. For example, between January 1963 and January 1966, P/Es averaged about 19. Yet stocks racked up average annual total returns of almost 16 percent.

In the early 1960s, P/Es were undeniably high. Investors were paying more for stocks' earnings. But they were well-rewarded for doing so. Ignoring the market just because stocks had high P/Es would have meant settling for savings account or bond yields of less than 4 percent.

More recently, in late 1986, P/Es climbed to thirteen-year highs of 18. Aficionados of "value investing" rang warning bells that the end was near for stocks. They were wrong. Stocks climbed another 35 percent. And indeed, even after the 1987 crash they never again got as low as they were at the end of 1986.

Ironically, by the time of the 1987 crash, I suspect, many of the doom and gloomers had lost their fear of high P/Es. But that is exactly when P/Es truly were high in both relative and absolute terms.

One particularly well read adviser I know, who is, incidentally, also one of the brightest and most thoughtful in the business, abandoned his earlier value-based cautious stance and loaded up heavily on blue chip stocks just prior to the crash of October 1987. Fortunately, he picked good stocks, so neither he nor his clients got scalped. But it took him a long while to recoup his losses.

THE "REAL" P/ES

Lessons like the ones above have convinced many financial experts that using P/Es to time the market is futile. That's why few use P/Es in practice, even though they pay lip service to them.

I admit that using P/Es alone as a market timing tool is a prescription for trouble. But P/Es can give accurate timing signals. All you have to do is put them into context by taking the economy, and especially inflation, into account.

As I've shown in earlier chapters, stocks' potential for growth depends largely on the economy—specifically, the potential for sustainable, noninflationary growth.

Like my other indicators, P/Es are almost worthless if they don't reflect the trend in inflation. This is why my favorite stock price value indicator is what I call real, or inflation-adjusted, P/Es.

Investors who use P/Es to time the market without looking at inflation are operating in a vacuum. They're like sportscasters trying to predict the success of a seven-foot-tall basketball player, without knowing what league he'll be playing in.

If the seven-footer were playing on a high-school team, for example, chances are he'd be a giant. With even a minimum of coordination, he'd score at will. In fact, our seven-footer would probably set all kinds of league records.

But if our seven-footer were in the National Basketball Association, he'd have to have exceptional talent to score; sheer height wouldn't be enough to get him by Michael Jordan, Charles Barkley, or other superstars who are quick enough, heady enough, and skilled enough to set records. The bottom line: Being seven feet tall may guarantee success in high-school basketball, but it doesn't come close to it in the NBA.

I suspect you get the analogy. A P/E of, say, 12 will virtually guarantee you success in stocks over the next twelve months, if there's no inflation at all. But if inflation is running at 8 percent annually and P/Es are at 12, the "real" P/E is really close to 20. This means it'll be hard to make money in stocks. In fact, you're almost guaranteed mediocre returns.

The point is that inflation really determines whether or not a P/E is too high (stocks are near a top) or too low (stocks are near a bottom). In other words, our benchmark for judging whether P/Es are too high or too low is stocks' worst enemy, inflation.

Many investors who preach the value of P/Es were blindsided by the market's meltdown in 1987 simply because they didn't consider inflation. They stayed clear of stocks in early 1987 because they mistakenly thought P/Es were too high. The P/E of the average S&P stock had risen from 17 to 23.

But in fact, inflation was still very low during the early part of 1987. So "real" or inflation-adjusted P/Es were lower than they were four years earlier, when stock prices were much lower. Inflation had been falling in early 1987, so stocks still had room to rise. The top was still a long way off, despite the fact that P/Es seemed very high to the naked eye.

Only later in the year, after inflation had risen from less than 0 percent to more than 4 percent, were stocks vulnerable. At that point, inflation was too high to support the market's high P/Es, i.e., investors' optimism for growth. And a crash was in the offing.

If investors had considered P/Es—not by themselves, but in the context of inflation and economic growth—they would have ridden the market to big profits in early 1987 and gotten out in plenty of time to avoid the losses of autumn. Again, in determining whether stocks are expensive or cheap, the absolute level of P/Es is not the important thing to watch. It's how high P/Es are relative to the current rate of inflation. In other words, "real P/Es," or P/Es plus the rate of inflation, are the key.

REAL EXPECTATIONS

P/Es reflect investors' expectations for companies' earnings growth. But real P/Es signal whether those expectations are realistic. If real P/Es are low, then stocks almost always rise over the next twelve months. If they're too high, stocks always nosedive.

Remember our economic train. Stocks can rise the most when the economic engine is running slow. That's because the economy has the most room to increase its rate of growth without sparking inflation. Low real P/Es indicate a slow-moving economic train, one with potential for big increases in growth without inflation. That's why low real P/Es always precede big upmoves in stocks.

With this in mind let's revisit the mid-1960s when stocks "mysteriously" kept rising although P/Es were high. Back then, inflation was low, so real P/Es (P/Es plus inflation) were low, too. This is why stocks were able to keep rising.

On the other hand, stocks usually peak when the economic engine is running fast. That's because the train can't speed up much more without overheating. In fact, it will probably have to slow down, sending stocks cascading.

High real P/Es signal a fast-moving economic train, one with limited potential. That's why they always precede big down moves in stocks.

Consider the mid-1970s again. Back then, stock prices fell even though P/Es were low. That's because inflation was high in the 1970s, so real P/Es were actually high.

THREE BUILDING BLOCKS

Now for the big question: What exactly is a real P/E?

I use three components to calculate real P/Es. First is the average price-to-earnings ratio of the S&P 400 stock index. This is simply the most recent value of the index divided by the past twelve months' earnings of the four hundred companies on the index.

I use the S&P 400 index because it's the best average of blue chip industrial stocks. Compared with all other indexes, it's been the most reliable in terms of reflecting the fate of the broad market. And it best reflects what's happening with the stocks most people own.

Unlike the Dow Jones Industrial Average, the S&P 400 is weighted by market value, so larger firms, the ones more people own, carry more weight than smaller ones. Also, the Dow contains only thirty stocks, hardly a representative sample of the market as a whole. The S&P 500 stock index, which most advisers use as a stock market gauge, includes stocks like utilities, which often tend to reflect bond market developments.

GPAs and P/Es

For statistics buffs, here's an easy way to understand the basic reasoning behind our real P/Es concept.

Suppose you are the admissions director of a university. You must decide which prospective students would excel if admitted, and which will not. Just as stocks are evaluated using P/Es, students are evaluated according to their grade point averages (GPAs). But your feeling is that the past GPA is really not that important in evaluating a prospective student's performance. Instead, you're more interested in students' GPAs relative to how much time they spent on their studies, a "real GPA" if you will.

In other words, you believe that a student's raw ability, not the amount of effort he or she puts in, is the critical factor for success in college. And the less time a student spent studying relative to the grades he or she made, the more raw ability that student has.

To determine how much time a student put in, you have just one other piece of data available to you: how much time the student has spent playing pinball. It's no surprise that the more time a kid has spent pretending to be "Tommy," the lower his or her grades, just as stocks' value is lowered, the greater inflation is.

Now you need to put all this information into a single number that represents a student's overall ability. For the sake of our example, let's assume that the range in grades and in hours of pinball per day are roughly the same.

You assign a number for each grade, with A=1 as highest and E=5 the lowest. At the same time, you assign a number for the hours per day spent playing pinball. Again, a 5 indicates the highest number of hours per day playing, 1 the least.

To arrive at a single number, you would add the number of hours spent playing pinball to the number corresponding to a student's average grades. In other words, if a student spent 5 hours a day playing pinball and maintained an A average, he or she would have a total score of 10, perfect.

Take a look at how this works. Suppose two students both have the same grades, say a B. Both would receive 4 points under your system. But one kid spends 2 hours a day at the pins, the other 5. Clearly, the one who spends more time fooling around is getting the same grade with less work. His score on our system would be a 9, the other would have a score of 6.

GPAs AND P/Es (CONTINUED)

Of course, for this system to work, your assumption that effort doesn't count must be right. And you'll also have to assume that students do nothing but play pinball or study. In other words, any time not spent studying is spent playing pinball and vice versa.

By adding scores together you get our measure of real GPA, which, if our assumptions are correct, will have a much better chance of correlating with future success than GPA by itself. (For you stat buffs what we have really done is create a new statistic which perfectly correlates with GPA less expected GPA.) Now if you substitute P/E ratios for GPA and inflation plus a dab of growth for the pins, our analogy is complete.

In the case of P/Es and CPPI the relationship is exceedingly strong. (Again for you stat buffs, the long-term CPPI explains nearly 70 percent of the variability in P/Es. That's a tremendous amount.)

The S&P 400 P/E is reported weekly in *Barron's* "Market Laboratory," under the heading S&P Industrials. Note that the reported P/E for the S&P 400 is based on the last twelve months' (trailing) earnings rather than forecasts for the next twelve months. There are hundreds of brokerages, research houses, newsletters, and so forth that make their living estimating what companies' future earnings will be. Many are quite good. But none is infallible.

Estimating earnings involves making numerous assumptions. Because these assumptions are based on economic forecasts, most earnings projections are notoriously inaccurate. And revisions can be astounding, particularly when predictions of economic growth and inflation are well off the mark.

In contrast, current P/Es are rarely revised significantly once they're announced, which makes them far more reliable. Combined with the other indicators in this book that gauge potential for sustainable economic growth, P/Es will beat Wall Street's earnings estimates hands down every time.

The one drawback with using the published earnings figures and P/Es is that occasionally they can be skewed by one-time events. For example, in the late 1980s and early 1990s many companies underwent extensive restructurings, streamlining and refocusing their organizations. Others adjusted their books to reflect new accounting regulations.

As a result, many firms were forced to write off millions of dollars in mostly non-cash expenses. This depressed their profits and sent their P/Es skyrocketing. But because many of these writeoffs were only one-time events, stocks were not as overvalued as their high P/Es made them seem. In that case, the high level of P/Es painted a misleading picture about how overvalued stocks really were.

Major restructurings don't occur very often. But to guard against drawing the wrong conclusions, I always use a variation of earnings in my model: cash-flow–adjusted profits. It's calculated by the following formula: 1.87 + .0466 times total corporate cash flow (in billions). For example, if the figure is $460 billion, adjusted earnings are about 23.3.

Cash flow figures are published by the Department of Commerce in hundreds of billions of dollars. They're released with every new report for gross domestic product (GDP). They can be found either on the report or in *The Wall Street Journal* the day after quarterly GDP numbers are released. Another source is *Survey of Current Business,* on page C-4, series 35.

Figures released are annualized for the quarter in which GDP is released. But don't worry about that. You can just plug the numbers released directly into my formula.

If you don't want to take the trouble to do cash flow calculations, published P/Es will work nicely most of the time. But when they're considerably above or below normal, adjusting earnings for cash flow provides an essential reality check.

The second component of real P/Es is inflation. The best measure is our old friend the All Commodity Producer Price Index. This index, as I showed in Chapter 1, does the best job of tracking multiyear trends in inflation—the ultimate arbiter of how sustainable economic growth is. Again, I prefer to use the five-year moving average of the All Commodity PPI (see Chapter 1) to smooth out short-term fluctuations.

In addition to P/Es and inflation, I've added a third component: earnings growth. The idea is that the faster earnings have grown, the less the potential for ever-faster sustainable growth.

Recall the economic train again. The slower earnings are growing, the faster they can increase at a sustainable rate without triggering inflation. The faster they grow, the less they can increase without inflation.

You can figure the earnings of the S&P 400 companies for the past twelve months by dividing the value of the S&P 400 index by its P/E. For example, if the S&P 400 index is at 400 and the index P/E is 20, S&P earnings are $20.

Next, you must find the percentage change in earnings over the past five years. To do this, divide earnings for the most recent twelve months by what they were five years ago. Again, as I said above, it's more reliable to use figures for cash-flow–adjusted earnings, rather than published earnings, in your calculations.

Now let's put these three variables together. The first step is simply to add the five-year average annual rate of change in the commodity PPI (inflation) to the P/E of the S&P 400. For example, suppose the S&P 400 P/E is 16 and the five-year average annual rate of change in the All Commodity PPI is 2 percent. The result is 18.

S&P 400 earnings growth, however, is not as important as either inflation or P/Es in determining what real P/Es are. Consequently, it carries less weight.

To give earnings the correct weighting, you must divide the percentage change in earnings over the past five years by 50. For example, if earnings have risen 50 percent during the past five years, the result will be 1.

Now you're ready to add all the numbers together. In our example, you'd add 1 (the adjusted earnings growth) to 18 (the sum of P/Es and inflation), for a total of 19. That's the market's real P/E.

P/E ratio for S&P 400
+5-year moving average of All Commodity PPI
+5-year percentage increase in S&P 400 earnings divided by 50
=Real P/E ratio for S&P 400

ONE GREAT INDICATOR

Once you understand all of the above, you're ready to tap into and understand one of the most reliable market indicators—real P/Es. And you'll know something even the most stalwart "value" investors don't: when P/Es are really too high to sustain a bull market's advance, and when they're so low that almost any stock will pay off big twelve months down the road.

The table "Real P/Es and the S&P" shows real P/Es' track record as a stock market forecaster since World War II. The first column shows the range of real P/Es. The second shows the twelve-month performance of the S&P 400 following those readings.

The results are truly staggering. Invariably, the higher the real P/E, the worse the market performed over the following twelve months. The lower the real P/E, the better stocks did.

For example, all three times that real P/Es have been above 24, the stock market has entered a bear market, dropping 10 percent or more. The average loss: 11.31 percent. Stocks have closed ahead for the year only three of the thirty-two times real P/Es have been above 23, and never by more than 7 percent. The average loss: almost 8 percent.

Equally awe-inspiring is real P/Es' incredible record at picking stock market bottoms. Since World War II, whenever real P/Es have been below 14, stocks have rallied an average of 34.1 percent in the follow-

REAL P/Es AND THE S&P 400

Real P/Es	S&P 400
Greater than 24	−11.31
Greater than 23	−7.82
22.5 to 23	−5.34
21 to 23	+0.07
17.5 to 21	+8.34
14.1 to 17.5	+17.11
Less than 14	+34.11

Average performance of S&P 400 for next 12 months at different levels of real P/Es.

ing twelve months. And at no time in history have stocks failed to rally strongly when real P/Es have been below 13.8.

With regard to our above example, the real P/E of 19 that we calculated is generally in the bullish range. Given a real P/E of 19, stocks have risen about 8 percent on average over the next twelve months. The best advice, therefore, would be to hold whatever shares you own, but to be selective in buying more.

HOW HIGH IS TOO HIGH?

Why do P/Es always seem to "max out" when they reach the low 20s or so? The answer relates back to dividend yields, which, like P/Es, are also a measure of value. That's because dividends are paid from earnings. They rise over the long term as a company's profits rise.

Stocks' prices rise as investors become increasingly bullish about the prospects of the underlying companies. At the same time, their P/Es rise and dividend yields fall. Just as a rising P/E indicates rising expectations, so does a falling dividend yield.

The key question is, at what level do investors' expectations for a stock or stocks—as reflected by dividend yields and P/Es—become unrealistic? The answer: Look at how many years it would take earnings growth to push dividends up to the level of current bond yields.

Long-term bond yields, as you recall from Chapter 4, roughly reflect corporate America's expectations for long-term annual economic growth (inflation plus real growth). The faster growth is expected to go, the higher the interest rate that companies are prepared to pay to borrow money to finance future growth. Consequently, higher bond yields correspond with faster economic growth.

The higher stocks rise, the further dividend yields fall. So, the longer it will take for an investor's yield to catch up to bond yields, or expected annual earnings growth.

How long is too long? No matter how you slice it, whenever dividend yields dip in the area of 2 percent, the wait is probably going to be at least fourteen years. That's just too long, given the kinds of uncertainties inherent in any complex economy. In other words, when more time than that is needed, the market almost always corrects.

In contrast, whenever dividend yields rise to 5 percent or more, the wait is always less than eight years. With that kind of risk/reward ratio, stocks always rally.

Because P/Es rise when dividend yields fall, they tend to peak out at about the same time dividend yields bottom out. That's why stocks almost never rally further after P/Es have risen to the low 20s, the time horizon is just too long.

SECRETS OF SUCCESS

Why are real P/Es such successful forecasters? Because they're never high enough to be in the danger zone unless some combination of the following occurs. First, investors go berserk bidding up stocks based on unrealizable expectations. Second, inflation is too high to support the kind of economic growth that investors expect. Third, earnings growth is running at an unsustainable pace and is due for a slowdown. Regardless of which combination of the above proves to be true, the result is always bad for stocks.

Conversely, real P/Es are almost never extremely low unless the following occurs. First, investors are less than optimistic about stocks. History shows that low expectations are the hallmark of every bull market's beginnings. Second, inflation is very low. Third, low P/Es indicate that earnings have been growing at a very slow rate. These last two events indicate that the economic train is only just leaving the station. The potential for sustainable growth is consequently at a peak—the ideal economic climate for stocks.

Keep in mind that extreme levels for just one of the components used in figuring real P/Es can turn the whole equation negative. For example, suppose P/Es climb to 24. Unless both five-year inflation and five-year earnings growth are falling, stocks are likely to plunge.

Because investors are expecting more from stocks than they can deliver, the market is due for a big crash, despite the bullish economic situation. This happened in late 1961. Then, five-year inflation was only about 1 percent, and five-year earnings growth was in negative territory. But regular P/Es were sky-high at over 23. Investors were expecting much more than stocks could deliver. And at the slightest hint of disappointment—in this case a minor rise in interest rates and a confrontation between President Kennedy and the steel companies—stocks plunged nearly 30 percent in just a few months.

A LEADING INDICATOR

P/Es are important for one other reason: They tend to be leading indicators for economic growth, and therefore also for the other indicators discussed in this book. For example, a high level of P/Es indicates that unemployment insurance claims (UIC) are almost certain to fall.

This may sound confusing. But it's actually quite logical when you stop to consider that P/Es essentially reflect expectations for growth in corporate earnings, hence economic growth.

Extremely high P/Es are an excellent warning sign that the Fed has shoved the economic train's accelerator to the floor. The economy may not be running fast now, but barring a quick tap on the brakes by the Fed, it's about to boom.

Faster growth leads to falling unemployment insurance claims, rising commodity prices, declining real interest rates, and rapid growth in the money supply, in short, inflation, and all the elements for a downturn in stocks.

In other words, high P/Es are a sign that all of the other building block indicators discussed thus far in the book are starting to deteriorate. High P/Es are telling us that no matter how bullish a signal commodity prices or unemployment insurance claims are flashing now for stocks, things are about to take a turn for the worse. The other indicators will worsen, and the market will fall out of bed.

The table "P/E Relative to UIC" makes this point. As you can see, when P/Es have been high (over 18), unemployment insurance claims have fallen. That's great news if you're looking for a job. But it's lousy for the market, which always runs on empty and dies on full.

A recent example of how P/Es "predict" trends in the other indica-

P/E RELATIVE TO UIC

P/E	UIC
Greater than 18	−0.6
15 to 18	+6.4
12 to 15	+14.1
Less than 12	+3.6

tors came in late 1991. All of my building block indicators were bullish for stocks, except for P/Es, which were at historically high levels. Focused on recession myopia, virtually no one on Wall Street or in the mainstream media said what P/Es were telling me then: The economy was about to start upon a recovery and the market's upside was shrinking.

LIMITS TO GROWTH

Although high real P/Es tell us that stock prices are expensive and that economic growth is about to accelerate, i.e., stocks are in for a rapid fall, it's possible for investors to overanticipate faster growth. In this case, they would bid stock prices—hence real P/Es—sky-high, and it would take months for economic growth and inflation to pick up steam.

Such a scenario would make it possible for earnings to increase gradually until P/Es came back to normal levels and stocks were no longer overvalued. In that case, high real P/Es would simply be forecasting a holding pattern for stocks, rather than a swift decline. And after profits caught up with prices, stocks would be ripe for another advance.

Such a scenario however, is very unlikely for one main reason: Prolonged periods of slow growth are politically unacceptable. Sooner or later the political party in power will pull out the stops to get growth back on an upward track again, to bolster its chances of reelection. When that happens, interest rates and inflation will flare up and stocks will drop. Authorities' actions can be especially dramatic during election years.

In other words, even if economic growth does not accelerate immediately after real P/Es hit the danger zone, stocks are still headed for trouble. If real P/Es are high and growth accelerates on its own, stocks will plummet. If real P/Es are high and growth remains sluggish, the politicians will weigh in with tax cuts, more government spending, or more interest-rate cuts to get things going again. And stocks will plummet.

The bottom line: there's really no way to come out a winner by buying stocks when real P/Es are high. You're doomed no matter what happens. Ignore them at your peril!

THE REAL THING

Real P/Es will put you eons ahead of the so-called value investors for one basic reason: They directly compare the market's expectations of growth with its potential.

But remember, real P/Es are excellent at picking market tops and bottoms mainly because they're so closely tied to inflation. Consequently, they're good indicators as long as they accurately reflect changes in inflation, which sometimes don't become clear until you look at the other core indicators: commodity prices, unemployment insurance claims, money supply, and interest rates.

Buying when real P/Es are on the low end of the scale will always get you into stocks at relatively cheap prices. And selling when real P/Es are in the high ranges will safeguard you from just about any major disaster the market will inevitably throw your way.

But not even real P/Es will always do a great job in picking out stock market trends on their own, especially when they're in that middle range, between 17.5 and 23. In other words, regardless of whether the real P/E has been at 22 or 18, stocks have often performed just as well over the next twelve months.

Putting all of my core indicators together into a clear-cut forecasting strategy is how I became Wall Street's number one market timer. Now it's time you mastered the the same recipe. The next chapter outlines my method.

POINTS TO REMEMBER

1. Price-to-earnings ratios (P/E) are the best way to gauge how expensive or cheap a stock or the stock market is. They're calculated by dividing a stock's price by its earnings per share for the last twelve months.
2. P/Es are effective stock market forecasters when compared with the long-term trend (five years) in inflation and economic growth. The result is called real P/Es. The higher the market's average real P/E, the worse stocks have performed over the next twelve months.
3. Real P/Es are also good forecasters of future economic growth. Abnormally high real P/Es tend to forecast too-rapid economic growth, and worsening of inflation.

7

The Big Picture

I'VE ALWAYS BEEN A STATISTICS NUT. I guess that goes back to the 1950s, when I was a kid growing up on the northside of Chicago.

My passion at that time was baseball's hapless Chicago Cubs. I'd stay up late to listen to their away games on the radio. And I spent many a summer weekend hanging out at Wrigley Field to catch home games.

I knew all the players by heart. And every Sunday morning, I'd pore over their weekly stats in the paper: batting averages, home runs, RBIs (runs batted in), stolen bases, and so on. I literally memorized thousands of figures.

As I recall, the Cubs were never a factor in the pennant race. But they did have one bright spot: the great shortstop and future Hall-of-Famer Ernie Banks. And I followed his career with true devotion.

As any baseball fan knows, the sport's highest honor each season is to be named most valuable player. One player from each league is selected for this award, based on a vote by sportswriters around the country. The winners are deemed to be the most indispensable to their teams in their respective leagues.

Banks's career reached its apex in the 1958 and 1959 seasons, when he won the RBI crown and was voted the National League's most valuable player twice in a row.

On the southside of town, another man was voted most valuable player of the American League in 1959, the gutsy second baseman Nellie Fox. Unlike Banks, Fox didn't really lead his league in anything, though his team, the Chicago White Sox, won the American League championship.

As a stats watcher, I remember being extremely disillusioned. If my beloved Ernie Banks was voted National League MVP on the basis of his strong individual stats, how did Nellie Fox win? After all, he didn't lead the league in anything. Shouldn't the American League MVP be chosen according to the same criteria as the National League MVP?

That's when it dawned on me that numbers by themselves really can't tell you the whole story about anything. They only make sense when you look at them in relation to the big picture. In other words, the other numbers. Or, in the case of both baseball and the stock market, other statistics.

Players are awarded the MVP title of their leagues because they are deemed to be the most indispensible player in that league for a given year. Fox and Banks both met that criterion, but for very different reasons.

Banks had far and away the National League's best individual season. In other words, his outstanding individual statistics made him the most indispensable player in the National League, and earned him the MVP award.

What made Fox indispensable, however, were not his great statistics. It was the fact that he was the leader on the team that won the American League championship, the Chicago White Sox. His leadership was vital to that team's great season. The vital statistic that won him the award was that championship.

At the same time, no one else in the American League really had a super year, as Banks did in the National League. In Banks's case, the team that won the National League title in 1959, the Brooklyn Dodgers, had no real standout leader.

It wasn't so much the statistics for one player that determined who won the MVP award. It was how they fit together with the team and the league as a whole. Sports is full of examples of individual statistics being rendered meaningless, except when considered as part of the whole. The Detroit Pistons of the National Basketball Association put together two consecutive world championships without a single real superstar in 1989 and 1990.

It's just that way with the stock market. The whole is always more than the sum of its parts. You can get bogged down in mountains of statistics, memorizing hundreds of facts and figures, and never really understand what's going on. Knowing how everything fits together is the key to success.

ABOUT SYSTEMS

If you've learned anything from this book, I hope it's that inflation is the key to understanding stock market trends. The higher the rate of inflation, the worse stocks tend to perform. The lower it swings, the bigger the profits from stocks. As a result, for any stock market timing system to really work, it's got to be closely related to inflation.

I've pointed out five key building blocks for predicting the relationship between stocks, economic growth, and inflation: commodity prices, unemployment insurance claims, interest rates (real rates and the short-term/long-term interest rate spread), real P/Es, and the money supply (M1 and M2 growth). Each building block is closely intertwined with growth and inflation. As a result, each verifies the others. So we can understand why they work, as well as how well they work.

Each indicator does a fine job of forecasting the market on its own. Even if you follow only one of them, year in, year out, you should reap profits that will make the pros blush. But as I've pointed out in each chapter, no single one of these indicators has a perfect record for forecasting market moves. Your profits will be much greater if you put each indicator in context with the other four.

The goal of this chapter is to show you how all five of these indicators fit together. The result is an excellent numerical projection of how much the stock market will gain over the next twelve months. It's the system that's made me the number one market timer for the past five years.

Obviously, the easiest time to forecast the market is when all five of our key variables are pointing in the same direction, i.e., are either bullish or bearish. Then your success is practically guaranteed.

That was the case in early 1991, for example, right on the eve of the Persian Gulf War. All five were ravingly bullish. Commodity prices and interest rates were dropping. Unemployment insurance claims were rising, real P/Es were low, and the money supply was growing at a moderate pace. The market went on to score a gain of more than 30 percent in the next 12 months.

Conversely, in August 1987, when my friends were dithering about selling their Connecticut farmhouse, all five of these key indicators were in the negative column. Commodity prices and interest rates were ticking up. The money supply was rapidly contracting. Real P/Es were high and rising. And unemployment insurance claims were dropping like a stone. The Dow plummeted more than 1,000 points over the next four months.

Unfortunately, the market rarely gives you such clear signals. In fact, more often than not, some of the indicators will be flashing bullish signals, while others are warning of a stalking bear.

How do you know which indicator is the most important to follow when two or more conflict? As I've pointed out, commodity prices tend to be the most reliable individual stock market indicator of the five, because they are the rawest expression of inflation.

But even a good showing by commodity prices does not guarantee a bull market, any more than a poor showing locks in a bear market. Just as in the determination of baseball's most valuable player award, hitting the most home runs doesn't necessarily take the prize. The key is how all the indicators fit together. And to know that, you've got to compare all of them simultaneously, through an equation. That's the basis for my system.

A SINGLE EQUATION

Coming up with my equation was no easy matter. It involved dozens of statistical calculations, such as regressions and multiple regressions. The result is a forecast of the market's percentage gain over the next twelve-month period.

The forecast is rarely right to the percentage point. But it does give you a sure-fire indication of what stocks will do over the next twelve months. I'm really not exaggerating when I say it's never missed a major market move.

There's no smoke and mirrors with my system. You don't have to be a genius to use it. In fact, anyone with a decent 386-chip computer, a Lotus spreadsheet, and a good statistics textbook can repeat my work in a few weeks, and probably improve on it, too.

What I did was find out how much of the variation in stocks was explained by each of the five indicators independently of the other indicators, or when all of the others remained the same. For example,

I found out how much variation was explained only by changes in unemployment insurance claims, and not by the other four indicators. Then I weighted each indicator in the equation, based on the results.

For example, as I've explained, changes in commodity prices on their own forecast stock market moves better than any other indicator. But what I did through my regression analyses was find out exactly what they explained about stock market moves that no other indicator did and then weighted it in the equation accordingly.

Finally, I added all of the weighted indicators together. The end result is a single number that is a pretty darn good prediction of how much the market is going to go up or down in the next twelve months. For example, if the result of the equation is plus 10, it means the S&P 400 should rise in the neighborhood of 10 percent over the next twelve months.

BUILDING BLOCKS

The best way to explain my weighting of the indicators is to take them one at a time. First, commodity prices, which have the best sole record of forecasting market swings of any of my indicators.

The key question to answer is how much of a move in stocks does, say, a 1 percentage point move in commodity prices trigger, assuming all the other indicators stay the same? In other words, if commodity prices rise 10 percent over a twelve-month period, where and how far can we expect stocks to move? Down 5 percent? Up 10 percent?

My analysis shows that the relationship between stocks and commodity prices can be explained by the following equation:

9.88
− (0.56 × the change in commodity prices for the previous 12 months)

= Projected 12-month change in stock prices

Suppose commodity prices rise 10 percent over a twelve-month period. To project stocks' performance over the next twelve months, you would first multiply 0.56 times 10 (the percentage change in commodity prices) to get 5.6. Then subtract 5.6 from 9.88 to get a twelve-month projection for stocks of plus 4.28 percent. In other words, when commodity prices have risen 10 percent over a twelve-month period, all else being equal, stocks have risen an average of just 4.28 percent over the following twelve months.

Note that the equation is completely consistent with what I said about commodity prices in Chapter 2. Falling commodity prices imply good returns, and rising commodity prices lousy returns. For example, if commodity prices have been falling by 10 percent, then the equation goes as follows: $9.88 - [0.56 \times (-10)]$. The result, a not-too-shabby average gain by the S&P 400 of 15.48 percent! (Remember, when you subtract a negative number you end up with a positive number.)

Of course, an equation using only commodity prices is not nearly as accurate as if you add in the other variables. In March 1980, for example, commodity prices were rising at a double-digit year-over-year clip. But unemployment insurance claims were also rising rapidly. It turned out that when you looked at both building blocks—and the others as well—you had to conclude that the market was poised for a big rally, not a fall. That turned out to be right on target. Stocks zoomed more than 20 percent in a few months.

If we add unemployment insurance claims to the equation, consequently, the results will be much better. Again through regression analysis, I've found the equation that works the best for using both commodity prices and unemployment insurance claims is this (note that the weighting for commodity prices is lower than before, to reflect the addition of another variable):

8.70
− (0.44 × the last 12 months' change in commodity prices)
+ (0.19 × the last 12 months' change in UIC)
_____

= Projected 12-month change in stock prices

For example, let's say commodity prices have fallen 10 percent over a twelve-month period, and that unemployment insurance claims have risen 10 percent over that same period. The result of the equation will be as follows: First, multiply 0.44 times the 10 percent drop in commodity prices to get −4.4. Subtract it from 8.7 to get a result of

13.1. (Again, remember that when you subtract a negative number, you end up with a positive number).

Second, multiply the 10 percent rise in unemployment insurance claims by its weighting of 0.19 to get 1.9. Finally, add 1.9 to 13.1 to arrive at a projection for stocks' performance of 15 percent for the next twelve months.

Rising unemployment insurance claims are good for stocks. Falling claims are bad. That's why falling claims reduce the projection for stocks and rising claims increase them. Meanwhile, rising commodity prices decrease projections, while falling commodity prices increase them.

When the commodity prices and unemployment claims send off conflicting signals, commodity prices carry more weight. But if the signal from unemployment claims is stronger, then they'll tilt the projection in their direction.

For example, if commodity prices fall 10 percent (a bullish sign) and unemployment claims fall 10 percent (a bearish sign), the projection for stocks will still be a good one. But if commodity prices fall just 1 percent and unemployment claims fall 30 percent, stocks' projected twelve-month performance will be just 3.44 percent. In other words, cash would still be your best bet.

I have done the same thing for the other three key indicators: real P/Es, money supply, and the interest rate indicators. These can be calculated exactly as I explained in earlier chapters.

I also made two other adjustments that need some explanation. To simplify the interest rate indicators, I used only the real interest rate indicator (long-term AAA bond yields minus CPPI inflation) discussed in Chapter 4.

For money supply growth, I use one indicator based on monthly M1 money supply growth, rather than M2 money supply growth as discussed in Chapter 5. M1 is a better indicator for the stock market than M2 because of its narrower focus.

To calculate the money supply indicator for my system, I take the "absolute value" of the difference between average monthly M1 money supply growth for the past twelve months and the forty-year average monthly change in M1 money supply growth. Absolute value means that no matter which of the two variables is greater, we still treat the result as a positive number.

To calculate this variable, I simply subtract the forty-year average of monthly M1 growth from the current monthly rate of growth. For example, if the forty-year average of monthly growth is 0.2 percent and the current average monthly change in M1 for the past twelve months is 0.3 percent, the value of this variable would be 0.1 percent. As the example below shows, I then multiply this result by a weighting of 29 and subtract it from the equation.

Now for the tricky part. Suppose that the average monthly change in M1 over the past twelve months was 0.2 percent and the forty-year average rate was 0.3. The result of the equation would still be 0.1. That's because we're looking for the absolute value of the difference between current monthly M1 growth and the forty-year average of monthly M1 growth.

Remember, money growth is like a river. Too much or too little flow is harmful for the economy and the stock market. Only a steady flow can guarantee success.

The faster M1 is growing, the better for stocks, up to a point. That point is what my money supply indicator is designed to measure. That's why we subtract it from our equation, rather than add it in.

For example, suppose M1 were growing at a 5 percent monthly rate, as opposed to a monthly average rate of just 0.2 percent. That would clearly be too fast for healthy economic growth. And our indicator would tip us off. Essentially, we'd have to subtract 29 times 4.8 percentage points, or 139.2.

Finally, note that the weightings of the equation have changed. Particularly, commodity prices in our final equation have only a 0.30 weighting, as opposed to their 0.56 weighting when they were considered on their own. The reason for the lesser weighting may seem complicated, but it's really a function of two basic rules of statistics.

First, commodity prices best explain market swings by themselves or when all other indicators are held constant. But other indicators reflect many of the same things they do. These statistical "overlaps" are weeded out when we view all of the indicators together.

Also, commodity prices are more volatile than other indicators, for example, real P/Es. Their smaller weighting takes this into account by making volatility less important. The end result is that commodity prices' relative weighting in the equation is much lower than they would be if considered all by themselves.

Real P/Es, on the other hand, carry the equation's biggest weighting. That's because they're the only indicator that measures how stocks are valued by the market. On their own, they're probably a less effective forecaster than commodity prices. But in the equation, they have far less statistical overlap with the other indicators than do commodity prices. And they're less volatile. That's why they draw a higher weighting.

One final point: the individual weightings in my equation can change fractionally over time. However, changes will not affect the accuracy of the forecasts.

83.78
− (0.30 × the 12-month change in commodity prices)
+ (0.28 × the 12-month change in unemployment insurance claims)
− (3.68 × the S&P 400 real P/E)
+ (0.85 × real interest rates)
− (29 × [the absolute value of the difference between 12 month average monthly M1 growth and 40 year average monthly M1 growth])

= 12-month projected change in S&P 400

Suppose that over a twelve-month period, commodity prices fall 10 percent and unemployment insurance claims rise 10 percent. At the same time, the market's real P/E is 14, real interest rates are 3 percent, M1 has averaged monthly growth of 0.1 percent for the past 12 months, and the forty-year average of monthly M1 growth is 0.2.

The resulting 12-month projection for stocks would be calculated as follows:

83.78
− (−3.0) [0.30 × (−10)]*
+ 2.8 (0.28 × 10)
− 51.52 (3.68 × 14)
+ 2.55 (0.85 × 3)
− 2.9 (29 × 0.1)

= 37.71 percent projected 12-month gain for stocks.

* *Remember*: When you subtract a negative number, it's the same thing as adding a positive number.

In other words, it would be a great time to buy stocks. And this bullish projection is completely consistent with what I've said so far in this book. All five of the indicators are generally bullish. Unemployment insurance claims are rising. Commodity prices are falling. Real P/Es are comparatively low, interest rate indicators are favorable, and the money supply is flowing above its long-term average, but nonetheless at a steady, manageable rate. All five core indicators, in other words, are generally bullish.

Now let's take a different example. Say our figures for commodity prices, interest rates, money supply, and unemployment claims remain just as bullish. But that real P/Es soar to 27, the extremely overvalued "danger" zone. In other words, stocks are at much higher levels. The twelve-month projection for stocks would now be a huge loss of over 10 percent. It's time to flee for the exits!

TRADING RULES

The results of my equation aren't perfect. But they're pretty close. The table "The System that Works" shows how well its projections have correlated to market moves over the past thirty-five years.

When this equation forecasts blockbuster gains of 30 percent or more, the market has always rallied at least 20 percent. The average gain was nearly 35 percent in the following twelve months. In stunning contrast, when the forecast is for a loss of 20 percent or more, the

THE SYSTEM THAT WORKS

Predicted 12-Month Change in S&P 400	Avg. Gain/Loss S&P 400	Months	Number of Months that S&P 400 Was Higher 12 Months Later
Greater than 30	34.98%	29	29
20 to 30	23.31	47	46
10 to 20	14.86	94	84
0 to 10	6.96	142	110
−10 to 0	−5.15	97	29
−20 to −10	−15.75	24	0

Five-indicator model forecast vs. average gains/loss in S&P 400.

market has always, without exception, fallen on its face. The average loss: a bonecrushing 29.2 percent.

Of course, there were only two such dire cases. But even when the forecast was for a much more moderate loss of between 10 and 20 percent, the market has declined without exception. The average loss: almost 16 percent. As the table makes clear, the results are exactly what you'd expect from an exceedingly accurate stock market forecasting model.

The bottom line is that basically any trading rule to buy when the projections are high and to sell when they're low will likely throw off big gains. The key is, the higher the projections, the greater your odds of scoring big gains. The lower the projections, the greater the chance of a bear market.

The table "One Great Trading Rule" shows how a hypothetical

ONE GREAT TRADING RULE

Indicator Was Bullish		Number of	S&P 400		
From	To	Months	From	To	% Change
Aug '54	May '59	57	31.26	62.09	+98.6%
July '60	Nov '61	16	59.25	74.72	26.1
June '62	May '64	23	58.32	85.79	47.1
May '67	May '68	12	99.59	107.00	7.4
May '70	April '72	23	83.16	121.30	45.9
Sept '74	Jan '76	16	76.54	108.50	41.8
Nov '79	June '81	19	116.10	148.70	28.1
Oct '81	July '83	21	134.00	188.32	40.5
April '84	March '87	35	178.57	334.65	87.4
Nov '87	Aug '89	21	288.00	396.53	37.7
Aug '90	Jan '92	17	390.79	493.00	26.2
Number of Months in Market		260	Compounded Gain		4700%
			Average Annual Gain (When Positive)		19.6%

investor would have performed by adhering to a straightforward trading rule. The rule I chose was to buy stocks whenever our model predicted year-ahead gains of at least 10 percent, and to sell whenever year ahead losses of 1.5 percent or more were forecast.

The results speak for themselves. As of early 1992, my rule would have kept you in the market for 260 months (out of a total of 456) during the past thirty-eight years. During that time, investing in the average S&P 400 stock would have netted you a nearly fifty-fold return on your money. With dividends, gains would have been almost 100 to 1. Including the interest you would have earned on your money when you were out of the market, the gains are about 200 to 1. That means $10,000 plunked down back in 1954 would have turned into about $2 million by early 1992.

Your annual gains while invested in the market would have been 19.6 percent. Including dividends, returns would have been almost three times those of a simple "buy and hold" strategy.

And there's nothing rigged about this trading rule. Any similar rule would work just about as well, which is precisely what defines an accurate forecasting system.

Yes, this stuff really does work. And to apply it you need access to a public library, a $5 calculator, and the time it takes you to read this book. That kind of investment in time and money will indeed put you many steps ahead of almost all the professionals in this business.

OTHER SYSTEMS

That in a nutshell is my system for mastering the market. I'm quite confident that if you use it faithfully, you'll be richly rewarded with enviable profits for years to come.

But the real strength of my system is not necessarily what kind of profits you'll make in a given year. It's that, if you follow my rules, you'll understand exactly why you're making money that year. That makes it infinitely more valuable than a system that may make you money one year but has no understandable rationale.

I think it was the great mathematician John Von Neumann who said that you don't understand something unless you can explain it to a ten-year-old. (Since my oldest child is eight, I have yet to use this criterion.)

In my system, each of the five key indicators has an easy-to-understand relationship to inflation, and hence stocks. For example, commodity prices, as we explained in Chapter 2, are the rawest expression of inflation. Consequently, it's easy to understand why my system works, as well as how well it has performed.

Unfortunately, the same can't be said of most of the hundreds of other systems available. Undeniably, many appear to work, scoring big returns at least for a time. But unless they can explain why they work, they're of little value to investors. In fact, if you rely too much on such a system, you can lose your shirt.

How many times have you read about or even followed one "system" for beating the horses, stocks, or anything else? Almost uncannily the system continues to work. But there's no real reason why. Eventually, something goes wrong. And since you don't know why the system worked in the first place, you certainly don't know why it's not working. In the end, you'll probably go broke.

Such systems may work simply because of the so-called law of large numbers. In other words, there are enough people out there with "systems" that some are bound to work for at least a while. But eventually, they almost always turn out to have no predictive power whatsoever.

For example, consider this experiment. There are millions of trees in the world. Every fall these trees lose their leaves. Suppose every September you put a basket under each tree. Then, every autumn for the next thirty years you count the number of leaves that fall into each basket. You now have leaf count figures for millions of baskets, for the past thirty years.

Now say you compare data for each basket with stocks' performance over that thirty-year period. Most of the baskets' leaf counts won't correlate at all to stocks' performance. But the sheer number of baskets means that several, perhaps only a fraction, will. In other words, changes in the number of leaves counted from these trees will correspond closely to changes in stock prices.

Undeniably, these trees' leaf counts would have been good market forecasters. The problem is that there would be no rational, understandable reason why. Consequently, there would be no real reason to expect that their leaf counts would continue to be good forecasters.

The same thing goes for any indicator that investors follow but don't really understand. In the stock market, this was certainly true of Joe Granville in the late '70s and early '80s, and was to a lesser extent true of Robert Prechter in the mid-1980s. Both "gurus" had indecipherable systems based on "waves" and "charts," with uncanny records. But there was no real reason why these systems worked. As a result, while lucky for a while, they were doomed to failure. Granville's comeuppance came in the early 1980s. Prechter's came with the crash of 1987.

Granville and Prechter weren't charlatans. They were just lucky. Lucky in the same sense that a guy can get hot at the crap table and keep winning and winning.

As my father always used to tell me, nothing, providing it's logically possible, is impossible. Maybe there are magical trees. But if you're going to use any stock market timing system, any indicators you use must be simple and always verifiable. In other words, make sure that the relationships that define the model make sense, satisfy basic laws of logic, and appeal to your intuition as to how things work in the world.

If you're going to follow leaf counts as an indicator for stocks, for example, make sure you know why they work. It might be true that the tree was located in the center of the most productive agricultural land in the country. There might be some biological basis for saying that the number of leaves a tree sprouts during the summer is related to the health of the soil. And, of course, you would have to show that the level of production on the land where the tree grew was related to overall economic activity and hence to the stock market.

In other words, there would have to be a slew of testable relationships that showed how the number of fallen leaves was related to market changes. It is never enough to say something works because it works. Such systems as Granville's and Prechter's turn out only to prove a variation of the law of large numbers, namely, that if you have enough systems, some are bound to work.

That's what truly sets my system apart from most others. The relationships don't depend on so-called cycles, wave patterns, or anything else you can't understand yourself without a supercomputer. Everything you need is at your fingertips and is based on simple relationships that (hopefully) can be understood by a ten-year-old.

OTHER SYSTEMS

Another question may occur to you. Are there other variables that could be included to improve results even further?

We live in a world with an infinite number of numbers. That means there will always be more ways of explaining things than there are things to explain. To point out relationships based on about forty years of stock market history, for example, I've had to analyze data about rates of change in stock prices for 480 months. Clearly, if I have 480 or more variables I can "explain" the rate of change in each and every month. For example, one of my rules might be: Every June of years ending in 55, the market gains 19.13 percent over the following twelve months.

And we would have 480 such rules, each one precisely explaining what happened to the market in each of the 480 months we were explaining. The trouble is, these rules would have no explanatory power whatsoever. Would there be any reason to suspect that the market would again climb 19.13 percent between June 2055 and June 2056?

This example may seem farfetched. But it's exactly what most so-called technical analysts do with their brainless talk of waves and other nonsense. In fact, I'll wager that some of these guys have more trading rules than there are stocks traded.

I think you see my point. To have any chance of explaining anything as opposed to just describing things, you've got to restrict the number of variables. That's the main reason why I've boiled my system down to five indicators: commodity prices, unemployment insurance claims, real P/Es, money supply, and the interest rate indicators. They don't explain everything. But they do a better job of explaining and predicting stock market moves than any other five indicators.

My system, however, is not without its drawbacks. Because it attempts to forecast stock market moves twelve months in the future, its signals may take weeks, or even months, to be borne out. And unless you're careful, you might find yourself giving up on them.

I know. I've been close to that many times. It's hard to stay bullish, for example, when the market keeps going down in spite of the indicators. Conversely, it's tough to stay cautious in the final manic days of a bull market.

Getting through those tough times is the subject of the next two chapters. In Chapter 8 is a discussion of what to do when the market over- or underperforms my system's projections. Chapter 9 shows how to cope with the most difficult psychological situation of all for investors: the crisis-sparked market meltdown.

POINTS TO REMEMBER

1. The five key signals to my forecasting model are: commodity prices, unemployment insurance claims, real interest rates, money supply growth, and real P/Es.
2. Each signal, while important on its own, is weighted by what it adds to the model that's not also reflected in the other indicators.
3. My trading rule is to buy stocks whenever my model projects a gain of at least 10 percent and to sell when the model forecasts losses of at least 1.5 percent. The strategy has reaped an average annual gain of 19.6 percent since 1954, nearly three times that of a simple buy-and-hold strategy.
4. With my system, you'll always know why you're making money, because it's based on understandable relationships. Information needed to calculate it is at your fingertips.

8

Market Timing for the Nineties

THE GREAT CHESS CHAMPION EMANUEL LASKER ONCE SAID, "If you see a great move, look for a better one." That's excellent advice for any endeavor, including stock market forecasting.

By itself, the system described in Chapter 7 has a very strong record. But as the 1990s have unfolded, I've discovered two related variables that improve the overall performance of my model in a big way: unexplained gains, or UG, and unexplained slack, or US. You can get great results by following just the five indicators from the last chapter, or even by tracking just one of my indicators, such as commodity prices. But to explain the stock market of the 1990s, US and UG provide an invaluable edge.

Unexpected gains, or UG, is the amount by which stocks have under- or overperformed the projections of my system over the most recent three-year period. In other words, it shows how stocks actually performed relative to what you would have expected them to do based on my five core indicators.

The idea behind UG is simple. When stocks have performed better over the past three years than my system has indicated, it's a bad sign. That's because stocks have probably moved up too much and are likely to do worse than my system currently forecasts, all things being equal.

Conversely, if stocks have done worse than my system has projected over the past three years, this is a good sign. Again, all else being equal, we then expect stocks to do better in the next twelve months than my system currently projects.

Unexplained slack, or US, is slightly more complicated. It's designed to measure slack in the economy that's not reflected in the other four monetary/economic variables: commodity prices, unemployment insurance claims, M1 money supply growth, and real interest rates. As I explained in Chapter 1, the stock market runs best when the economy is growing at a sustainable pace. As long as there's enough slack to allow growth to speed up without igniting inflation, the market will generally continue to move higher. Once the slack tightens up, stock rallies tend to fizzle. Used in conjunction with the other four variables, US tells us definitively how much room the economy has to run before stock market investors should start bolting for the exits.

WHY UG AND US ARE IMPORTANT

You might be asking yourself why we didn't explain UG or US in an earlier chapter. The reason is that both variables are significant only when you consider them within the context of the five core indicators—commodity prices, unemployment, interest rates, money supply, and real P/Es.

For example, how the stock market has performed in the past is virtually unrelated to what it will do in the future. But stocks' past performance is very significant when you consider it relative to my forecasting system, through UG.

This sports analogy should help explain just what I'm driving at. Suppose a college coach wants to find the best way to choose high school kids for football scholarships. Again and again, he has found that the heavier team usually wins by a lot. He has also noticed that a team of straight-A students usually beats a bunch of D students. But in this case, the final scores are usually very close. So he decides to pick a team based solely on weight. After all, he reasons, a team of straight-A students is no match for a bunch of 250-pounders.

But his team of heavyweights posts a loser season and he begins to get threatening letters and phone calls from the school's alumni.

What's wrong? His conclusion is logical, but his reasoning is flawed. This coach has got to consider how important grades are, given two teams of equal weight. If he keeps one of the variables constant (weight), he can accurately judge how important the other variable is (grades).

Assume the coach starts seeking heavy students who also get A's.

His final score is not usually as lopsided as when his big guys played little guys. But he's now winning most games.

What the coach has learned is that weight and grades tend to be inversely related to each other—when one goes up the other tends to go down. That's because most students with high grades tend to weigh less than those with low grades.

The only reason grades didn't show up as more important initially was because when selecting smarties, the coach was more likely to choose lightweights. And because weight is more important than grades, it seemed that grades hardly mattered.

As he found out, the real test for how important grades are is to compare teams with the same weight but different grades. It turned out the big smart team beat the big dumb team every time.

How does all this relate to picking stocks, US and UG? As I said, past market performance by itself is not important in predicting stocks' future. As such, it's exactly like "grades" in our football example. By itself it doesn't seem very important. But when we hold all the other variables constant, it turns out to be very important. The same goes for US.

The message is that anyone who's interested in finding a sound forecasting system must go one step further than answering the question "What's the relationship?" Rather, the final question is: "What's the relationship when you hold everything else constant?" Grades proved to be very important only when the coach compared teams of the same weight. In the same way, past performance proves to be a very important indicator for forecasting the stock market. But this emerges only when, in a statistical sense, you hold all the other variables constant.

CONTEXT IS KEY

Because UG is essentially the past performance of the market itself, relative to what we would have expected stocks to do based on my forecasting model, it's useful to market forecasting, while market performance by itself is not.

Sure, there's a small tendency for big gains or losses to be reversed, or "corrected." But the relationship is not that strong. In other words, let's say in the past two years the market has climbed by more than 50 percent. If you knew nothing else, your best bet would be a down market over the next twelve months. Similarly, if stocks had dipped 10 percent in the past three years, the better bet would be for them to rise in the following year, providing you knew nothing else.

But that's not always the case. In fact, there are many cases of people going broke by basing their investment strategy on the market's past performance. Take the 1980s, for example. Stocks rallied year after year, confounding the bears who were sure that the market's gains were guaranteeing a bear market lying in wait. Or look at the 1970s, when the market's continuing losses were equally baffling to the bulls, who were sure that prices had to stop falling.

Only when you put past performance into the context of my core indicators is it a different story. In relation to these variables, the market's past gains and losses can tell us a lot about where stocks are likely to go in the future.

If real P/Es were only 14, for example, a 50 percent gain by stocks in two years may be less than we would have expected. Odds are that stocks would stage another sharp rally during the next twelve months.

I hope that by this time I've made the point clear. Past market success by itself is not a real indication that a bear market lies in store. Stocks' failure, by itself, does not clearly point the way to a bull market. But when you consider past market performance in light of what core economic indicators are saying, it becomes very important, just as grades become very important when comparing teams of equal weight. The bottom line: UG can dramatically improve the performance of our model.

In our equation, UG is the market's actual gains or losses over the past two years minus our system's forecast for stocks over the past two years. The key is whether UG is above or below what our forecasting system has indicated.

For example, suppose that all the conditions for a bull market are in place over a two-year period: real interest rates are high, real P/Es are low, commodity prices and unemployment claims are dropping, and the money supply is rising at a moderate rate. On average, the market has done extremely well historically under such conditions. So your expected gains will be relatively high for that two-year period. After all, these conditions would mean that some combination of high growth and relatively low inflation is prevailing.

But suppose stocks' performance during that two-year period was far higher than what our system forecast. What does this mean?

In this example, the stock market had a very high unexpected gain, or UG. Consequently, although our system's forecast for stocks over the next twelve months is exceedingly bullish, we would expect stocks to underperform this forecast.

NO SMOKE AND MIRRORS

Like my five core indicators, UG also makes theoretical sense. Remember the "magical trees" we debunked in the last chapter? The point I made is that if you have enough trees and enough baskets you are bound to find several whose leaf counts relate to changes in the stock market. In other words, these trees will seem to "predict" changes in the stock market, although there will be no discernible reason for it.

False indicators and phony market timing systems always give themselves away because of one fatal flaw: There are no verifiable relationships to back them up. That's in no way true of UG, or unexpected gains.

How do we know that UG has a real relationship to the market and that it's not just a meaningless coincidence? By the other relationships that follow in its wake.

If UG is high, for example, it's a sign that corporate earnings are likely to increase over the next twelve months. After all, higher-than-expected stock prices mean that corporate earnings are bound to increase more than expected. As a result, high unexpected gains also mean that economic growth should be higher than expected in the following year.

How this relates to stocks is simple. When actual stock market gains have been higher than what my system has forecast, UG is a positive number (actual gains or losses minus forecast gains or losses). This means that the economy is set to run faster. Unemployment insurance claims and real interest rates are likely to fall, while bond yields and commodity prices will probably rise. All these results are bearish indicators for stocks. As a result, when UG is high, i.e., the market has gained more than our indicators would have suggested, it's a sign that stocks have gotten ahead of themselves. That's why a high UG tends to be a negative for the market.

Remember our economic train? When the engine is running slow and cool (earnings are growing slowly and stock prices are down), stocks have the most room to run. That's when they typically stage their best performances. But when the economy is running fast (earnings and stock prices are rising), the market typically peaks and hits the skids.

In conclusion, when UG is high, it's a clear sign that the economic train is starting to run too fast. Under such conditions, the Fed is almost certain to slam on the brakes to fight inflation, usually by raising interest rates. And that's bad news for stocks.

On the other hand, when UG is low or negative, it's a certainty that the economic train is only beginning to pull out of the station. Stocks will soar.

WHY US IS IMPORTANT

Unexplained slack, or US, is an indicator that's become especially important in the unique economic environment of the 1990s. The early 1990s were marked by two major trends: The economy was able to grow for a very long period without igniting inflation, and stocks traded at record-high market valuations (see Chapter 6) with very little volatility. Both of these factors were missed by my five-indicator system, but my unexplained slack, or US, indicator anticipated them nicely.

US was able to succeed because it took one factor into account the others didn't, a problem that was basically unique to the early 1990s: The extreme weakness of the U.S. banking system. During the 1980s, banks and savings and loans were freed from many of the Great Depression era regulatory safeguards that had kept them out of more risky ventures in real estate and other enterprises. As a result, they plunged into making new riskier loans and entering deals they thought would reap massive returns.

Unfortunately, their timing couldn't have been worse. Many banks were already feeling the pinch when the recession hit in 1990. As real estate values slipped and less creditworthy businesses failed, banks' and thrifts' earnings and reserves plummeted, driving some into bankruptcy and pushing others to the very brink of destruction. This left the Federal Reserve with only one choice: Pump up money supply growth to help the banks work their way out of the crisis.

Starting in late 1990, the Fed opened the floodgates, speeding up M1 growth to almost banana republic levels. Under normal conditions, this money river would have flowed through into the real economy within a matter of months. In practice, however, the result was quite different.

Wary of making major new loans with their finances so weak, banks instead used their newly replenished reserves to buy low-risk Treasury securities. This quickly boosted both reserves and earnings, since the lack of new loans kept the economy weak and created further downward pressure on interest rates. Though lending across most of the country did start to pick up by late 1991, falling rates continued to encourage banks to buy still more bonds rather than make loans well into 1993. As a result, the economy remained weaker than it would have otherwise been. That additional economic slack, in turn, kept the stock market moving higher much longer than it would have under typical conditions.

MEASURING US

Obviously, history never replays itself exactly. Based on their checkered track records, I fully expect banks to continue to make bad loans, and occasionally to get themselves into major jams. The real estate crisis of the late 1980s and early 1990s, for example, came right on the heels of the Latin American debt crisis of the early 1980s, when U.S. banks made huge, risky loans to even less creditworthy borrowers abroad. But because economic slack could conceivably come from many different places, I use a more generic, two-part indicator to measure US, which gives an excellent indication of unexplained slack whatever its source.

The first component of my US indicator is the twelve-month rate of change in long-term bond yields. As I explained in Chapter 5, there is no reliable correlation between stock prices and long-term bond yields. There is, however, a strong and verifiable relationship between economic growth and bond yields. Basically, when there's a lot of slack in the economy, there's no inflation and bond yields tend to fall. When slack starts to tighten up, bond yields rise in anticipation of faster inflation. Bond yields' continuing plunge from late 1990 through mid-1993 was one of the best indications that there was still plenty of economic slack to support continued rises in stock prices.

Bond prices and yields, of course, also respond to myriad other factors in the short run, especially psychological ones. To smooth out the bumps, I use bonds' twelve-month rate of change, in other words, where yields stand now in relation to year-ago levels. In addition, to eliminate the effect of credit risk, I use yields on twenty-year AAA bonds. This data can be found in *Barron's,* the *Wall Street Journal* and also the Commerce Department's monthly *Survey of Current Business* as "High Grade Corporates," page C-5, series 116 (see Appendix).

The second component of US is basically relative rates of money supply growth. The idea is to get a grip on how much money from Fed pump priming is getting through to the real economy, thereby generating growth, tightening up slack, and ultimately putting an upside cap on stock prices. The two money supply measures for comparison are the sixmonth rate of change in M2 and the 12-month rate of change in the narrower M1.

As I explained in Chapter 5, M1 and M2 money supply measures tend to mirror each other over time. The way they measure economic slack together is timing. Basically, M1 is the rawest measure of the money supply, comprised of only the most spendable, or "liquid," types of money such as checking accounts and currency in circulation. M2 on the other hand, includes less liquid forms of money, such as savings accounts and bank certificates of deposit.

Generally, greater inclusion makes M2 a better indicator of what's happening in the real economy, whereas M1's relative narrowness makes it superior in gauging the Federal Reserve's latest moves.

During most economic recoveries, boosts in Fed-stimulated M1 flow through within a matter of a few months to M2. Consequently, M2 growth starts to catch up with M1 growth. Conversely, when the Fed tightens M1 growth, M2 growth tends to follow suit as the economy slows down.

In most cases, the difference between M1 and M2 growth will be slim and not too revealing of economic slack. That was not the case, however, in the early 1990s. Banks' unwillingness to make loans kept money out of the economy. Meanwhile, falling bank interest rates induced investors to plow money into stocks and bonds to beat bank rates. As a result, M1 grew by leaps and bounds while M2 stagnated. It was a clear tipoff of the large amount of slack in the economy. Historical data for both M1 and M2 growth are available in many places, as Chapter 5 points out.

Putting the money supply growth and bond yield components of US together, I've come up with the following formula:

+ 12 × 12-month average monthly change in M1
− .26 × ([12-month percentage change in AAA-rated 20-year bond yields] + [6-month average monthly change in M2 growth × 20])

_____

= Unexplained Slack, or US

For example, suppose bond yields fell 10 percent during the past twelve months, M1's twelve-month average monthly rate of change was 1 percent, and M2's six-month average monthly rate of change is .5 percent. The value of US would be +12. In other words, there's a lot of economic slack out there that will not be picked up by the other variables in our model. And this slack adds 12 percentage points to our projected gains for stocks over the next twelve months. You can see that this makes sense in our example. Bond yields are declining despite rapid growth in M1, while M2 is only half as great as M1 growth.

As with UG, US makes perfect logical sense. It's no "magic tree" indicator. The stock market runs best on empty, i.e., when prospects for faster economic growth without inflation are best. That's precisely the time when there's a lot of economic slack, and when US's value and impact will be the greatest on our overall model. Conversely, the market runs worst on full, when the economy is already running at a rapid clip and further bursts of speed are likely to ignite inflation. That's when there's the least amount of economic slack out there, and when US's impact will be the least on our overall model.

HOW US AND UG WORK

Now it's time to see how US and UG fit together with the rest of my system for effective market timing in the 1990s. The new model is written below. Note that the weightings are slightly different from those listed in the last chapter. (This difference allowed us to simplify a bit. For UG we just use the two-year rate of change in stocks rather than the actual definition, which is the two-year rate of change less the projected change.)

94.19
- − 0.29 × 12-month change in commodity prices
- + 0.21 × 12-month change in unemployment insurance claims
- − 4.18 × the real P/E of the S&P 400 Stock Index (P/E plus inflation in commodity prices)
- + .77 × real interest rates
- − 33 × the absolute value of 12-month average monthly M1 growth − its average monthly growth over the past 40 years (always expressed as a positive number)
- + .09 × average monthly M1 growth over last 12 months
- − .13 × the S&P 400 Stock Index's two-year change (which is what we have defined as UG)
- + 12 × average 12-month M1 growth − .26 × 12-month rate of change in AAA bonds − .26 × 6-month average M2 growth × 20 (which is what we have defined as US)

= predicted 12-month change in stocks

Let's reconsider the first example of the last chapter. All the indicators mentioned remain the same: Commodity prices and unemployment insurance claims each fell 10 percent over the past twelve months. The S&P real P/E is 14. Real interest rates are 3 percent, and the difference between average monthly M2 growth for the past year and average monthly M1 growth for the past forty years is 0.1 percent.

Now let's add in UG and US. We find that stocks have gained about 50 percent more over the last two years. Meanwhile, twelve-month average monthly M1 growth has six-month average monthly M2 growth by a wide margin. The result is the following:

+94.19
−2.9 (0.29 × −10 percent)
+2.1 (0.21 × 10 percent)
−58.52 (4.18 × 14)
+2.31 (.77 × 3)
−3.3 (33 × 0.1)
+.009 (0.9 × 0.1)
−6.5 (.13 × 50)
+12 (which we got from calculating US)

= forecasted 12-month gains of 39.4 percent

Adding UG and US to the model adds more than 2 percentage points to our original projections. Why? Because the market's 50 percent two-year gain, while above normal and a negative, was more than offset by the twelve-percentage points US added to our projections.

The summary table "Our Best Model" is probably the best way of showing how effective this model is. Perhaps the most remarkable finding is that whenever our model calls for a gain of at least 30 percent—as it did in the above example—stocks have never gained less than 19 percent. In other words, a forecasted gain of more than 30 percent is as close as you can come to a guarantee of a major bull market.

Almost as impressive is the fact that the market has always returned at least 11 percent whenever my system has forecast a gain of 20 to 30 percent. This means that of the 87 times in which the model has called for a gain of at least 20 percent, the market has never failed to produce at least a solid advance the following year.

OUR BEST MODEL

Model Projection	Average gain	Months	Months Positive
Greater than 30%	32.6%*	36	36
20% to 30%	24.2**	51	51
10% to 20%	15.8	79	75
0% to 10%	6.1	156	117
−10% to 0%	−5.1	100	28
−20% to −10%	−15.9	20	0
Less than −20%	−25%***	3	0

* Worst case is 19%.   ** Worst case is 11%.   *** Best case is −21%.

With this kind of record, it's not surprising that virtually any commonsense trading rule based on this system will yield exceptional long-term results. The rule we chose to illustrate this point is to buy stocks when the system forecasts at least a 9 percent gain and to sell when it forecasts at least a 1.5 percent loss. As our table below shows, following this rule you would have realized an annualized gain of over 22.9 percent while invested.

A RECORD OF SUCCESS

Date From	Date To	# of Months	S&P From	S&P To	% Change
Jan '54	Sep '55	21	25.55	46.88	83
Jan '57	Jul '59	30	48.53	64.23	32
Oct '60	Oct '61	12	56.90	71.42	26
Jul '62	Jul '64	25	58.32	88.19	51
Aug '66	Jun '68	22	86.40	109.70	27
May '70	Feb '72	21	83.16	116.90	41
Aug '74	Feb '76	18	85.51	113.00	32
Mar '78	Aug '78	5	97.65	115.00	18
Apr '80	Nov '80	7	115.60	155.10	34
Nov '81	Jul '83	20	136.80	188.32	38
Jul '84	Mar '87	32	171.70	334.65	95
Nov '87	Sep '89	22	280.11	397.08	42
Apr '90	Jan '92	21	393.17	492.97	25
		256	Total Return		8100%
			Average Annual Return		22.9%

Rule: Buy when the model projects gains of 9 percent and up. Sell when the model projects losses of 1.5 percent or more.

ADVANCED FORECASTING

Remember what I said earlier. You can do quite well by sticking with the system discussed in the last chapter. So you don't have to use UG or US.

But if you do take the time to follow this sixth variable, your returns will be even better. And as Lasker, the great chess champ might put it, "that's the name of the game."

Of course, the greatest unexpected performances of the market are usually in response to bad news. These crisis-motivated self-offs can trigger devastating short-term losses. But for the savvy investor, they can represent fabulous buying opportunities. Taking advantage of these great market panics is the subject of our next chapter.

POINTS TO REMEMBER

1. The principle behind UG, or unexpected gains, is this: When the market has outperformed my projections for a three-year period, gains are likely to be less than what the model is currently projecting.
2. The principle behind US, or unexplained slack, is this: There are times when my other indicators don't fully reflect the slack in the economy. Bond yields and differences between measures of money supply growth should spot any slack they miss.
3. You don't have to use UG and/or US to be successful. But both would have dramatically improved your results thus far in the 1990s. Both are also constructed in such a way as to spot slack from any source. The average annualized gain for the model including UG and US is 22.9 percent.

9

What Goes Down Must Come Up

THERE ARE A LOT OF WALL STREET SAYINGS, most of which are full of hot air. "Buy when there's blood in the streets," however, is one worth heeding. In other words, the best time to buy stocks is after a big drop, when everyone else is afraid to.

I'd add one refinement to this: When the streets are crimson, you have to shut your eyes and buy with both hands. In other words, you have to ignore your emotions and jump in.

After a big drop in stocks (more than 10 percent on the S&P 400 stock index), the economic indicators I've described in earlier chapters are almost always bullish. That's because when stocks stumble hard, economic growth usually does too. But that's precisely when both the economy and stocks are likely to pick themselves up and take off.

I can virtually guarantee that if you carefully follow the economic indicators in this book, you'll make a mint in the market, long term.

But I also realize that none of us are automatons or live in a vacuum. We are emotional creatures. And big drops in stocks shake our confidence. No doubt about it.

When the market crashes hard, instinct screams at you to bail out. As stock prices fall, you'll be tempted to discard tried-and-true indicators and conclude that things are somehow different this time around.

I know. I've been there. But let me assure you. As long as the indicators in this book are bullish, stocks are going higher. Events may delay this, but they won't change it. If you hold on, you'll always be vindicated in the end. And if you have the fortitude to buy, rather than sell, you can make a killing.

That's not to say I don't dream about forecasting some of these setbacks, and thereby avoid the whole problem altogether. But since we're not gods, the best we can do when faced with crises is to keep our heads, and our faith in time-tested indicators.

CRISIS MENTALITY

When this book went to press, the most recent major sell-off had started in August 1990, after Iraq invaded Kuwait. And I was caught off guard by this, just like the rest of Wall Street and maybe even the CIA.

At the time, I had just correctly forecasted the market's minor drop from its July 1990 highs. And I was confident the market would recover because my indicators were then flashing green, despite what other analysts were saying about recession and inflation. In fact, I was considering buying more stocks when Saddam Hussein invaded Kuwait.

In the tense weeks that followed, even the strongest stocks plunged 20 percent and more. The Iraqi invasion left me in a quandary. All my economic indicators were flashing bright green. Meanwhile, the overriding political event—the invasion and Iraq's threat to world oil supplies—was pushing stocks the other way, straight down.

I realized that the 1990 collapse was very similar to the crash of October 1987, which also had me tied up in knots. Back then, my indicators had warned me of the drop, so my clients were high and dry when the storm hit. But after the crisis, amid all the apocalyptic chatter on Wall Street, my indicators were flashing green.

In both 1987 and 1990, I couldn't believe my eyes. How could these signposts that I had spent years developing be advising me to buy, when my gut was saying there's tremendous risk. What was wrong with them?

I remembered that after nights of pacing the streets of New York in 1987, I finally decided to cast my lot with the indicators. I held my nose and bought stocks. The final results were spectacular.

BIG DECLINES ARE BULLISH

Still, I needed more assurance in 1990 than my 1987 success. I began to take a long, hard look at all my indicators to find out if anything was wrong. Had some of them outlasted their usefulness? What was I missing? I pored over the data, sometimes staying up all night.

Finally, it dawned on me. To reassure myself, I had to go back in time and examine every sharp market decline since World War II.

Specifically, I looked at all the times that the S&P 400 index had lost 10 percent or more in a period of twelve weeks or less. I had two goals: (1) to find out what was going on economically during each of these periods; and (2) to find out what had happened to stocks twelve months after they hit bottom.

What I found was positively shocking. Since World War II, almost every major decline in stocks, like that in the fall of 1990, had ended with the same result: the beginning of a major bull market. My conclusion: Big drops in stocks are almost always screaming buying opportunities.

As I looked over my research on crises, I realized that the results merely quantified that simple maxim that legendary investors like J. Paul Getty and John Templeton had used to build their fortunes: "Buy when there's blood in the streets."

It's truly amazing how many investors fail to practice this simple rule. But then, I guess that's why so many fail in the stock market.

Some of my best friends, for instance, will wait patiently to buy a piece of land or a car until the price comes down. But they'll jump whole hog into a stock that's risen 50 percent at the peak of a bull market. And they wouldn't think of buying the same stock after it's fallen 50 percent at the bottom of a bear market.

IGNORE THE CROWD

During steep market sell-offs, the vast majority of investors—from pension fund managers in Manhattan to Granny in Ohio—are panic-stricken. They're convinced that whatever they own is destined to fall. Consequently, they maniacally try to unload their stocks at any price.

It's easy to see why. At such times, all the news in the media is bad. Many people have already lost thousands of dollars on paper, and stock prices seem to slip further every day. Moreover, every headline and most Wall Street analysts are putting a negative spin on even typical events.

All the so-called experts are spouting off myriad reasons why stocks are going to fall even more, and why anyone buying stocks is crazy.

Part of the reason the media go overboard is because they know that panic sells. But you can't blame the papers for everything. The main reason is that people are afraid to go against the crowd and to think for themselves. As a result, they're almost always on the sidelines, just when stocks are begging to be bought.

After a steep decline, the sellers have already sold. More important, the excesses are already wrung out of the market and the economy. The potential for sustainable economic growth, the manna of the market, is huge.

Sometimes the indicators go from bullish to extremely bullish, as in 1990. Occasionally, as in 1987, they go from extremely bearish to extremely bullish, just because of the huge crash itself.

Either way, stocks have only one direction to go—up. In such cases, savvy investors, with the guts to act contrary to the crowd, can then buy top-notch shares for a song.

Unfortunately, it's hard to keep your wits about you when everyone else is in a tizzy. Your broker, who makes his living off of commissions, may even try to talk you out of buying. Your friends and relatives will probably think you're crazy to be in the market, if you actually tell them what you're doing.

I also know this from experience. The market's drop in the wake of the Iraqi invasion of Kuwait unfortunately coincided with a newsletter conference in San Francisco where I was speaking. I was confident that the economic indicators were bullish. And armed with my research about market declines, I was sure that stocks' recovery was only a matter of time.

But even with all of my self-assurance, it was almost impossible not to feel a few pangs of uncertainty and self-doubt. I was almost the only optimist at the conference, engulfed by a sea of doomsayers. And these weren't stupid people.

The whole situation begged the question: Was I so much smarter and harder working than they? Or was I simply and unjustifiably wrong?

The bears at the conference, including the notorious Joe Granville, were positively gleeful to see me in this quandary. In speech after long-winded speech they derided my position and needled my newsletter's subscribers who stuck with me. Almost to a person, he and others predicted the Dow wouldn't finish the year above 2000.

One newsletter writer actually stopped me on the way to a speech to tell me why all the "evidence" was saying stocks were bound to fall more and that I was doing subscribers a disservice by being pig-headed.

At that same conference, there was also a bull vs. bear debate. But both the participants were died-in-the-wool bears!

I think most of the people who heard my speech that day were highly skeptical to say the least. But had they followed my advice to buy, and ignored the howling mob outside, they would have cleaned up.

Within a few months, the S&P 400 had done a complete reversal, bursting on to all-time highs and beyond. Small stocks staged one of their biggest rallies in history. Practically anyone with the courage to stand tall then was rolling in dough.

And almost all the bearish advisers at that San Francisco conference had dramatically switched to the bullish camp, including the theatrical Granville.

WHAT'S IN A DROP

Why are big drops in stocks almost always a good sign? First, enduring drops in stocks start with a whimper, not a bang. And they start when the economic news is good, too good.

That's because economic events that trigger major bear markets occur only over longer periods of time. It takes months, sometimes years, for a full-scale cycle to unfold: from recession, to growth, to inflationary growth, to recession again.

Since World War II, bear markets have typically started in the third phase, when economic growth triggers rising inflation. That's a sign that growth isn't sustainable. But it's precisely at that time that the economic news tends to be all good. So very few people expect a recession, only a continuous run of the bulls.

In contrast, the effect of a major political or economic crisis is immediate. The very week following Saddam Hussein's invasion of Kuwait, for example, stocks and bonds collapsed.

At such times, everyone and his brother expect a long-lived bear market. But these precipitous declines are almost always temporary. Unless you have the luck or clairvoyance to avoid such setbacks in advance, it's almost always better to hang on to your stocks through thick and thin. In fact, if you have any spare cash, you should use it to buy stocks by the truckload!

Consider what happened in January 1991 when the Persian Gulf crisis was "resolved," with the bombing of Iraq. In that short period, stocks rang up one of their largest one-week gains since World War II. Once again this proved that intense declines, whatever their genesis, sow the seeds of their own reversal.

The second reason big drops in stocks are a good time to buy is because they're usually caused by a crisis. Sometimes the crisis has an immediate economic effect. That was the case in summer 1990, when the Iraqi invasion spooked the oil market and scared consumers. Sometimes there's little economic impact, as with the Sputnik incident in 1957 (see table "Investing in Crisis" on page 121).

Either way, stocks come up shining after a crisis. When the crash has an immediate economic impact, as in 1987, it creates economic slack—the conditions necessary for growth to continue without triggering inflation. So, the market indicators show improved readings, and stocks take off.

When a crisis has little or no economic impact, as in 1990, stocks are beaten down for no fundamental reason. So, they're soon off to the races.

LESSONS OF HISTORY

In addition to the Persian Gulf crisis, there have been eight other major sell-offs since World War II. And I've found that each followed a pattern similar to that of the Persian Gulf ordeal.

The chart below shows what triggered each sell-off, how far the market fell, and how far it rose during the following six and twelve months. Note that I didn't include the Cuban missile crisis or the Kennedy assassination, because they didn't lead to significant market declines.

In each case, stocks started out overvalued, particularly in terms of price-to-earnings ratios. Many of these crises were political in nature, and some of these also had an economic impact. Some did not.

But all of the crises have several things in common. First, there was enormous economic slack after stocks dropped, and massive potential for noninflationary growth.

Second, stocks tanked because the market was looking for the absolute worst-case scenario to happen, not the most likely future. And this is another reason that major declines on average have been short-lived and led to great bull markets. Those with the courage to buy when there was "blood in the streets" have reaped massive gains.

INVESTING IN CRISIS

Crisis	Drop in S&P 400	6 Months Later*	1 Year Later*
Korean War, June 1950	−15% in 5 weeks	+31%	+36%
Sputnik, October 1957	−10% in 3 weeks	+8	+30
Steel Price Roll Back, April 1962	−20% in 8 weeks	+11	+24
Liquidity Crisis, May 1970	−12% in 4 weeks	+16	+42
Arab Oil Embargo, October 1973	−17% in 9 weeks	−1	−28
Nixon Resignation, August 1974	−19% in 5 weeks	+30	+27
Hunt Silver Crisis, March 1980	−12% in 4 weeks	+26	+29
Financial Panic, October 1987	−26% in 3 weeks	+7	+16
Iraq invades Kuwait, August 1990	−20% in 12 weeks	+28	+30
Average	−16.7 in 5 weeks	+17.3	+22.9

* Percentage change in S&P 400.

The average twelve-month gain on the S&P 400 stock index after these nine crises was nearly 23 percent. In seven of these cases, the gain was at least 24 percent. Percentage gains for the six months following each crisis are even more astounding: an average annualized gain of 37.8 percent.

Generally, the stronger the economy before the crisis, the shallower the drop and the steeper the recovery. In fact, the less a crisis had to do with economics, the more stocks tended to gain later on.

In October 1957, for example, stocks fell 10 percent in three weeks entirely due to panic about the Soviets' launching of the Sputnik satellite. Many thought that America was losing the technology race to the Soviets. Those who kept their heads cleaned up. One year later, when such overblown fears were a thing of the past, they were banking gains of 30 percent and more.

Ditto for the sell-off triggered by the federally ordered cut in steel prices in April 1962. Then, President Kennedy went to war with big steel and forced the major oligopoly to make steel less expensive. Many investors feared this was the prelude to socialism in the United States and sold stocks, which lost 20 percent in eight weeks.

Almost like clockwork, twelve months later panic sellers came to regret their emotional move. By then the steel magnates and the president had come to terms, and the stock market had risen 24 percent.

Some of the sell-offs were motivated by fears that a political crisis would bring about the economic conditions for a bear market. But once the political threat passed, so did the economic threat. And stocks recovered with a bang.

Several times, for example, events have led to fear of sky-high commodity prices. This is what happened in the first post-World War II crisis, the outbreak of the Korean War in June 1950. Back then, stocks dove 15 percent in five weeks.

Just as people feared Saddam Hussein would control world oil supplies in 1990, fear spread in 1950 that communism's advance would choke off world supplies of vital commodities. Commodity prices across the board soared, just as oil did in 1990. Panic-stricken investors bailed out of stocks en masse.

But when United Nations forces stymied the Communists' advance weeks later, the crisis passed and commodity prices returned to prior levels. Because none of the other conditions for a bear market were in place, stocks soared 36 percent over the next twelve months—one of the biggest one-year gains on record.

Other times the culprit has been fear of erratic or insufficient growth in the money supply. In 1970, for example, the market slid 12 percent in four weeks due to concerns about the dollar's strength—the so-called liquidity crisis. All of the world's currencies were pegged to the dollar, which in turn was pegged to gold. The resulting overhaul of this system led to a titanic 42 percent rebound in the stock market over the next twelve months.

The largest sell-off since World War II was the crash of October 1987. As we've discussed throughout this book, nearly all the economic warning signs for a bear market were in place before the decline began: slowing growth in money supply, skyrocketing commodity prices, falling unemployment, rising interest rates, and so on.

But the later stages of the drop—namely the 508-point fall in October 1987—took on political overtones. The market's concern was no longer about a bear market or an economic slowdown. It was the paralyzing fear of another Great Depression.

But this overblown fear sowed the seeds of the market's recovery. For if the economy was overheating going into the crash, it was subdued afterward. And, of course, stocks were much cheaper. The combination of cheap stocks and a slack economy invariably leads to a strong market.

When stocks hit bottom in 1987, some analysts were telling their clients to take money out of banks. Wall Street was full of apocalyptic "new depression" jargon for months to come.

But the threat was over. Just twelve months later, stocks were already 16 percent off their lows. And within four years, they were hitting new all-time highs, 20 to 25 percent higher than the 1987 top.

DOUBLE JEOPARDY

Only once have stocks failed to recover fully from a steep sell-off within a year's time: the period following the Arab oil embargo in

October 1973. But part of the reason that decline failed to prove bullish was the onset of another political crisis, the Nixon resignation in August 1974.

Richard Nixon was the first U.S. president ever to be forced out of office before his term expired. The political uncertainty surrounding his disgrace sent the recovering market into another escalating spiral of worry. After being buffeted 17 percent by the Arab oil embargo, stocks slid another 19 percent in five weeks.

The aftermath, however, was considerably more agreeable. The new wave of confidence that followed Gerald Ford's swearing in as president ended the political crisis. Stocks then staged their first signs of life in years, rising 30 percent over the next six months.

I can just hear you asking, "What about 1929?" The great market break in October 1929 heralded the start of the Great Depression. Right? Wrong.

As we showed in Chapter 5, the Depression did not begin with the crash in 1929. It started with a sharp drop in money supply that began in 1930, when our Rule of Three was flashing red.

Indeed, the crash of 1929 provided one of the great buying opportunities of the century. Between November 1929 and mid-1930 the market climbed a heart-warming 50 percent.

The *real* bear market began with a whimper in 1930, when the money supply shrank.

BUYING DECLINES

History tells us that practically any major drop in stocks is bullish. But getting the most for your money during such times isn't simple. Crises are inherently dicey times. Making a wrong move can cost you dearly.

Before you jump in whole hog to any weak market, run through the following steps.

1. *Don't buy after a more than 10 percent drop in stocks, unless the indicators are bullish*. This is by far the most important rule for profiting from crises. I've given you plenty of reasons why big declines

lead to very bullish conditions for stocks. I don't know of any cases when they haven't.

But if our forecasting model (see Chapter 8) isn't bullish in the aftermath of a major decline, I would still stay out of stocks, no matter how cheap they seem.

2. *Declines of 10 percent or more that occur over twelve weeks or less are most likely to lead to super bullish conditions.* Since World War II, this is the classic pattern that every major sell-off has followed. Longer-lasting declines are usually rooted in underlying economic problems.

Here's how to calculate the length and depth of a decline. Find when the highest price was reached by the S&P 400 before the drop started. Match this with the current price and date. For example, say the S&P was at 300 on July 15, but had fallen to just 250 by September 15. Essentially, the market would have fallen 16.7 percent in just eight weeks. Consequently, that would qualify as a rapid sell-off.

3. *Ascertain the reason behind the drop.* Most of the time, it's quite easy to pinpoint what has everyone worried. It's usually plastered all over the front pages of newspapers, argued about ad nauseam on talk shows, and generally blown way out of proportion.

Think beyond the current problem and imagine what will most logically happen after it's resolved. During the Persian Gulf crisis, for example, commentators constantly fretted about the costs of the "inevitable" ground war. Some speculated that Iraq could defeat U.S. forces.

But by far, the most likely outcome of the Persian Gulf War was a victory by the United States and its allies. Assuming this, investors could have expected stable oil prices and a slackening of inflationary pressures, and that these results would in turn have led to a sharp rebound by stocks.

That's not to say that you can always predict the outcome of crises. But every problem eventually gets solved. Fears about what might happen in a worst case are almost always exaggerated. And most important, the market beats stocks down because it expects that improbable worst case, so risks are low.

4. *Stick to quality stocks.* Only by buying top-notch stocks can you

be sure to capitalize on the market's rebound. They're low risk and have guaranteed growth prospects. Best of all, because the public sells off good and bad stocks alike in times of crisis, they're just as cheap as the market's cats and dogs.

During my speech in San Francisco back in fall 1990, I said no matter what the price of oil was tomorrow, people would still shave with Gillette razors, or buy General Electric lightbulbs, or eat at McDonald's. I still believe this. These companies will keep making money in almost any economic or political climate. And they're always among the first to recover from big declines. All three scored major gains during the bull market that followed the Gulf crisis.

The next chapter shows how to pick others like them. In contrast, many of the market's cats and dogs never recovered from the market's 1990 drop. Most of these scored only small gains, and with much higher risk to boot than quality stocks.

USE YOUR HEAD, NOT YOUR HEART

Buying stocks after a steep decline is probably one of the hardest things you'll ever do. But if you follow the rules I've laid down here, it could also be one of the most rewarding. There's no better time to reap windfall short-term gains with so little risk.

Sure, you'll face the ridicule of acquaintances who are brainwashed by the media. But then that's why stocks are so cheap at market bottoms. Near a top, the guys ribbing you are all mortgaged to the hilt in stocks.

Rest assured: As long as the core indicators are looking good, you can't be far off. Don't let sudden, major declines in stocks get you down. Keep the faith.

POINTS TO REMEMBER

1. Whenever the market has fallen more than 10 percent in ten weeks or less, it has almost always been a great time to buy stocks.
2. Sudden declines are bullish because they wring the excesses out of the market and the economy. That leaves more room for sustainable economic growth, and therefore leads to bull markets in stocks.

10

Picking the Right Stocks

IT'S BEEN SAID THAT A RISING TIDE RAISES ALL SHIPS. That's also true of the stock market. Even the worst companies tend to do well during a bull market. Even the best ones can slip a bit when the bear comes to call.

In other words, as long as you follow the market timing rules I've laid down in this book, you should enjoy sizable profits almost no matter which stocks you buy. You'll do far better, however, if you learn how to pick good stocks, and steer clear of the bad ones.

The stock market projections I've explored in previous chapters are all based on broad stock market averages, namely the S&P 400. Theoretically, if you could buy and sell all the stocks in the S&P 400 average in accordance with their signals, I'm confident you would make a mint year after year. More realistically, you can buy stock index futures, or one of the index mutual funds now offered.

But like any other market average, the S&P 400 contains both good and bad companies. The only thing they have in common is that they're big. So at any given time, some of the stocks will be on the skids, while others are soaring.

Therefore, you can dramatically improve your returns over my system's projections by picking the best stocks and avoiding the worst. A great stock will always outperform a bad one during a bull market. It will hold its own better than most during a bear market. And it will lead the charge back up the mountain when the bull reigns again.

Take the full-scale stock market panic of August 1990, for example. Then, the market was already down more than 10 percent from its July highs. And it was falling more every day as bad news continued to pour in from Iraq, concerning that country's invasion of neighboring oil-rich Kuwait.

In the previous chapter I mentioned speaking at an investment conference in San Francisco that very month. Attendees were frantic. Almost every other adviser at the conference was exhorting investors to sell all stocks in anticipation of the worst.

I, too, was having a few sleepless nights. Though the indicators in this book were unequivocally telling me to stay put and ignore the panic, it was tough to stay calm.

One of the things that kept me from taking leave of my senses was the basic soundness of my portfolio, and those of my clients. I held only stocks of great companies, Wall Street's finest. Regardless of what happened in the Persian Gulf, they were going to keep pumping out a rising stream of profits. Eventually, I knew, they'd soar far beyond even their previous highs.

And that's exactly what I told the conference attendees who came to hear me speak. As long as they held stocks of great companies, I maintained they had nothing to worry about. In the end, they'd be vindicated. "Take General Electric," I said. "People will still be using lightbulbs tomorrow, whether oil is at $5 or $50 per barrel. GE will still make money."

My advice proved to be right on target. Once the crisis passed, GE and other great companies led the market's charge to new heights. Those who hung on to them—or better yet who bought them after hearing me speak—were justly rewarded.

The ability of great stocks to withstand adversity is something you can count on through thick and thin. As I pointed out in the last chapter, you can't always protect yourself from the role of random chance in the market. No matter how certain you are about your research and the economic indicators, there's always the possibility of another crisis-related sell-off.

But barring the greatest calamity—a nuclear war, for example—the GEs of the world will survive and thrive. Regardless of who rules Russia, people will be buying these companies' products. Earnings will keep growing, and shareholders—though they may face some severe short-term pain—will prosper, as long as they keep their cool. And even in a bear market, some great companies' stocks will doggedly remain in an uptrend.

At the same time, even the best-laid market timing strategy can be derailed by picking a portfolio of dogs. If you pick bad companies, you'll reap only mediocre returns, no matter what the market does. And if stocks tank, there's no assurance your shares will rebound during the next rally.

In contrast, if you take the time to choose only great companies, you'll still be hurt when the market pulls back. But you'll be able to sleep easy in the knowledge that your stocks will lead the next bull charge up the mountain. No matter what happens, they'll keep you in the game.

Knowing how to time the market is the first key to long-term success in stocks. Picking good stocks is the second half of the story. And it's absolutely essential to stock market success.

BUY GENERAL ELECTRIC

What makes a "great" stock really great? Everyone seems to have his or her own idea. No matter where I appear at a public forum—radio, television, investment conferences—people are always asking me what I think about their favorite stocks. Many have quite sophisticated questions. And very often, they teach me something I didn't already know.

But what most of these questioners really want from me is confirmation that they've made a good purchase. And all too often, I simply can't tell them what they want to hear.

There are currently more than 4,000 stocks traded in North America, with thousands of others listed on overseas exchanges. The sad reality is that there are just too many choices for most investors. The vast majority simply have no idea how to go about picking great stocks.

Many have the mistaken idea that the only way to make money in stocks is with "insider information," or by "getting in on the ground floor" of some harebrained scheme. More often than not, they wind up outsmarting themselves, putting all too much of their portfolios into dogs that go nowhere while the market keeps going up.

How many times have you or someone you know bought a stock on the advice of a newspaper article, or a broker or friend, only to watch it nosedive. More often than not, investors in this trap ask themselves what went wrong, and wind up blaming whomever recommended the stock to them. But the real blame lies with them, for buying a stock they didn't understand themselves.

The irony is that it is relatively easy to pick great stocks. The legendary Peter Lynch was once asked how he managed to build Fidelity Magellan into the top-performing mutual fund of the 1980s. His reply was by doing nothing fancy.

I couldn't agree more. There's no smoke and mirrors involved. To find great companies, you don't have to get in on the ground floor, or have inside information. In fact, most of the greatest stocks out there are household names.

What I'm really saying is, you don't have to buy the "next General Electric" to reap ungodly profits from the stock market. All you really have to do—provided you use the market timing indicators I've laid down here—is to simply buy General Electric itself.

You don't have to believe me on that one. Just look at the truly great investors who have made billions by following this strategy: John Templeton, J. Paul Getty, Peter Lynch. Or the legendary Warren Buffet, the so-called Oracle of Omaha, who once said: "It's just not necessary to do extraordinary things to produce extraordinary results."

All of these guys were winners precisely because they didn't try to be heroes with every stock pick. They contented themselves with buying great companies at the right time. Then they watched their money grow.

DEFINING GREATNESS

What defines a great stock? Quality. And if quality is the key to greatness in stocks, then market dominance is the first key to quality.

A "dominant" company holds almost total control over a market, be it specialized toys or retreaded tires. Such control means little competition, which gives the firm freedom to price its product to keep up with costs. This ensures long-term earnings growth. General Electric, for example, is the world's premier maker of thousands of electrical components, machines, defense electronics, and other technology-based products.

Of course, a company may be the dominant provider of an obsolete product, or a product destined for an explosion in competition. In either case, its days as a quality company would be numbered.

For example, being the dominant provider of telex machines didn't stop Western Union from sliding into oblivion. U.S. Steel once reigned supreme over the American steel industry, only to be cut down to size by rising foreign competition in the 1970s. In the early 1990s, once-omnipotent computer giant IBM was forced to cut back and refocus operations to face a rising tide of competition.

That's why quality companies must not only be dominant in their industry, but their industry must have great growth potential as well. In other words, the company's products should occupy a niche that will be in high and rising demand, and which will not be threatened by competing interests. Such products could be positioned to take advantage of a social, economic, or political trend, or be based on a proprietary technology that no one else has, or else be in a market where no one else can afford to compete.

Sizing up a company's products in this way may seem complicated. But fortunately there's an easy way to tell simultaneously if a company enjoys a dominant market position and if its products should have successful future. Look at its profit margin: profits divided by total sales, expressed as a percent.

Truly dominant companies have profit margins that are close to ten-year highs and are in an uptrend. This signals that the company is actually increasing its market dominance, and its ability to generate an ever-rising profit stream.

A profit margin shows basically the firm's profit per unit sold. The higher the percentage, the more money the company has on hand to grow with. Dominant companies nearly always have profit margins that are dramatically higher than those of other companies in their industry. The less competition, the greater profits per unit of sales.

A rising margin indicates that the firm is squeezing an ever-rising profit stream from its business. That's almost impossible to do in the face of rising competition, which promotes lower prices. And it's equally impossible if a company's products are fading into obscurity.

Therefore, a rising margin is a sign of increasing dominance over a certain market.

The simplest way to tell if a firm's profit margin is rising is with a five-minute look at its latest quarterly or annual report. The key page is the Income Statement. Simply divide the line marked "net income" (usually at the bottom of the page) by the line marked "total sales" or "total revenue." If the result is greater than that for the previous year, the company's profit margins are rising.

For example, suppose that during a given year a company makes profits of $500 million and has total sales of $2 billion. Its profit margin would be 25 percent ($500 mil ÷ $2 bil). Now suppose it had profits of $400 million on sales of $1.9 billion the year before, for a profit margin of 21.1 percent. We can infer that the company's profit margin is in an uptrend, and thus that it's becoming more dominant in its industry.

Value Line Investment Survey, found at many libraries, also lists profit margins for many companies. In addition, the publication lists margins for prior years, as well as industry averages for purposes of comparison. The results may not be as accurate as if you do the calculations yourself. However, they're usually sufficient for purposes of comparison. Companies also usually publish statistical summaries. These list such data as profit margins, earnings, dividends paid, cash flow, debt, equity, and other items for previous years.

One thing to be aware of is that dominant companies aren't risk free. Any number of factors—poor management, changes in the economy, regulatory and legal snafus, or technological shifts, to name but a few—can knock them off their pedestals. But even if a dominant company does lose its way, the process will be gradual, not precipitous. Keeping tabs on how your stocks match up to the criteria I've listed here should give you plenty of time to bail out if need be.

Another possible pitfall is that these stocks can be overvalued from time to time. But if that happens, the effect will be only temporary. So even in the event of a crisis-sparked sell-off, when the indicators miss the market's move entirely, you can count on the stock's price to rise inexorably over the years. In other words, as long as you stick with these dominant companies, you'll eventually come out ahead, no matter when you buy them. That's true even if you have the misfortune to buy in at a market top.

For example, the period from summer 1990 to summer 1991 was extremely volatile for General Electric stock. At its peak in mid-1990, General Electric traded as high as $75 per share. By fall, the market's sell-off—triggered by the Iraqi invasion of Kuwait—had sent the stock reeling. Within weeks it finally touched a low of just $50 per share.

But shareholders of this steady grower were well rewarded for holding on. The company's dominance in electronics, defense contracting, and other industries kept profits rising. Finances remained secure and operating margins kept widening. When the market finally began to resurrect itself, GE stock was one of the first to recover, surging to new highs by midyear. Even those who bought at the 1990 top made money, if they held for the full twelve months.

STRONG BALANCE SHEETS

True dominance, as characterized by high and rising operating margins, is not the only criterion for quality companies to meet. They must also have strong balance sheets to help weather any economic storm in style. And it gives the firm strength to fight off competitive threats, should they arise.

I have two criteria for strong finances: low debt and high cash flow. Unlike most other expenses faced by a company, debt is a fixed cost on the balance sheet. Interest and principal must be repaid, regardless of how either the economy or the company's business is faring.

Dominant companies' market power means chances are slim that their debt won't be repaid. But if business is bad, expansion plans, such as strategic acquisitions of other companies, may be derailed by the need to repay debt from depleted levels of funds.

Also, high-debt companies must pay off their outstanding notes and bonds as they come due. That generally means refinancing by issuing more bonds. If interest rates are higher during refinancing than they were at the time the old bonds were issued, interest expense can rise and depress profits. Low debt, on the other hand, means low interest costs and enhanced flexibility to expand operations and pay off debt.

My rule with debt is, generally, the lower the better. But the optimum level of debt for an individual company can vary. Regulated utilities, for example, can support a higher level of debt than most firms, because of the high degree of earnings reliability they enjoy. Also, some faster-growing firms can sustain a higher level of debt than most slower-growing ones, provided their market power is growing (i.e., profit margins are rising).

These exceptions notwithstanding, I generally look for stocks with total debt of no more than one-half of stockholders' equity. Companies that meet this criterion should have no problem blowing over any potholes down the road, come what may. And they'll probably enjoy gold-plated credit ratings from such major services as Moody's and S&P. That means A3 or higher from Moody's or A− or higher from S&P.

To calculate this so-called debt-to-equity ratio, first turn to the balance sheet in the company's latest annual or quarterly report. Find the amount for Total Long-Term Debt. Divide it by the amount for Total Stockholders' Equity.

The result will be the debt-equity ratio, or debt expressed as a percentage of equity. Suppose a company has long-term debt of $1 billion and stockholders' equity of $2 billion. Its debt-equity ratio would be 50 percent, so it would meet our stiff criterion for quality companies.

One further point: Be sure to include only Long-Term Debt and to exclude Current Liabilities, which are included on some balance sheets under the Total Debt column. These are offset by Current Assets, so including them will give an artificially inflated figure for debt.

CASH IS KING

The second criterion for a strong balance sheet is high cash flow. Cash flow is the money the company pays its bills with. It includes earnings, plus any item that lowers a firm's profits but doesn't involve spending cash. In other words, to calculate a company's cash flow, you add back noncash expenses—such as depreciation or amortization of nonfunctioning assets—to earnings.

I consider cash flow to be high when it covers all of the company's capital costs, which include debt repayments, construction expenses, retooling of needed equipment, expansion costs, costs of complying with legislation, and so on.

Any cash a firm has beyond that point is considered to be "free cash flow." It can use this money for a variety of things: to buy back shares of stock, boost dividends, pay off additional debt, and/or make acquisitions. Any of these options are extremely bullish for shareholders.

The best way to calculate a company's free cash flow is to turn first to the "Statement of Changes in Working Capital." Unfortunately, many companies do not include this document with their quarterly financial reports. So you'll have to obtain their most recent 10-Q (published quarterly) or 10-K (published annually) form. Most firms will send these to anyone who asks for them.

Once you have the form, turn to the "Statement of Changes in Working Capital." This could also be listed as the "Condensed Statement of Cash Flows." Rather than add up all of the items that are comprised in Cash Flow, simply find the amount entitled "Net Cash Used for Investing Activities." Subtract it from the amount labeled "Net Cash Provided by Operating Activities."

If the result is positive, the company is generating free cash flow. If it's negative, it's not. For example, suppose that over a twelve-month period, a firm generated $2 billion in cash flow (net cash provided) and had $1.9 billion in capital spending (net cash used). It would have $100 million in free cash flow. On the other hand, if the firm had $2 billion in cash flow and $2.1 billion in capital spending, it would not have free cash flow.

Be sure to use periods of at least twelve months, in order to guard against being misled by quarterly fluctuations. It's also a good idea to compare results for the most recent period with those of a year earlier. If Net Cash Provided is increasing compared to Net Cash Used, the company is probably getting stronger.

Alternatively, *Value Line Investment Survey* also lists debt, equity, cash flow, and capital costs for many stocks. To calculate the debt-to-equity ratio, simply look in the box entitled Capital Structure, and divide the percentage figure for Long-Term Debt by the percentage figure for Common Stock.

The result will be a good approximation of the company's debt-to-equity ratio. For example, if the box lists long-term debt at 25 percent of assets and common stock at 60 percent, the company's debt-equity ratio would be 41.7 percent (25 ÷ 60).

For Free Cash Flow, look on the main page of the writeup and find the amount entitled "Capital Spending Per Share." Subtract it from the amount "Cash Flow Per Share." If the result is positive, the company is generating free cash flow. For example, if capital spending per share is $2 and cash flow per share is $3, the company is generating free cash flow of $1 per share.

Note, however, that *Value Line* figures are often approximations based on a specific formula. Consequently they may not take into consideration the idiosyncrasies of specific stocks or industries. Use them as a basis of comparison for picking stocks. But before you buy, get a copy of the company's financial statements, just to be sure.

STOCKS FOR ALL SEASONS

Stocks that meet the criteria I've described—that are dominant in their industry, have strong growth prospects, and issue a solid balance sheet—are the ideal candidates for employing the market-timing strategy I've discussed in this book.

If you search out and buy seven or eight different issues each time our economic indicators set off a buy signal for stocks, you should almost certainly do much better than our projections during bull markets. And even if you do get caught by a bear market, you could still score gains. That's the best way I know of to reap an ever-rising stream of profits for the rest of your life. Remember, look for rising profit margins, low levels of debt (less than one-half of equity), and free cash flow.

Of course, big stocks aren't the only way to win. Often small stocks do just as well, or better. That's the subject of our next chapter.

POINTS TO REMEMBER

1. Picking the right stocks is just as important to your investment success as timing the market correctly.
2. The best way to pick great stocks is to stick with quality: stocks with market dominance, consistent earnings growth, and solid balance sheets.

11

When It Pays to Think Small

IN PROFESSIONAL BASKETBALL, SIZE IS ALWAYS A BIG ADVANTAGE. Just look at a list of superstars for the past ten years: Kareem Abdul-Jabbar, Larry Bird, Magic Johnson, Michael Jordan. All of these gifted men have well above-average stature.

Only the truly exceptional "little" guy, like Isiah Thomas of the Detroit Pistons, routinely wins and wins big. And he's no shorty at six feet tall.

In the stock market things are different. In fact, the small fry usually roll up the biggest profits. Between 1926 and year-end 1990, the market's smallest stocks chalked up an average annual gain of 11.6 percent. In contrast, the S&P 400—the market's largest stocks—gained just 10.1 percent. And if your starting point is year-end 1932, the comparison is much greater, with small stocks averaging gains of 15.9 percent a year compared with 11.8 percent for big companies.

Put another way, an investment of $10,000 in a typical small stock at the beginning of 1933 would have grown to $81 million today. But it would have expanded to just $8.1 million if invested only in blue chip stocks.

Small stocks' main attraction is their superior growth potential. All of today's blue chips were once growth companies. I'll wager most of us have at least one friend who made a mint by buying IBM or Xerox when it was a small growth company. Maybe you did too.

Even if they never reach the big time, small stocks tend to outperform their larger cousins. That's because they have much more room to grow. It's like a five-feet-eleven-inch-tall adult who gains three inches in height. That's considered a major gain. In contrast, it's no trick for a baby to double in height in a short time.

Similarly, a company with $1 million in sales can double its size by boosting its revenue $1 million. But for a $100 million firm to double, it must increase sales by $100 million. Needless to say, there are many more ways for a $1 million company to add $1 million to sales than there are for a $100 million firm to double its revenue. Consequently, small firms can often sustain faster growth rates for earnings and dividends than large ones.

For all of their advantages, however, small stocks aren't always the best bets. First, small stocks as a group can lag the market averages for considerable periods. From January 1983 through December 1990, for example, the small fry scored an average annual return of just 2.6 percent, which was dwarfed by the big stocks' 14.6 percent average yearly payback.

Second, small stocks' prices are far more volatile than those of big stocks. They do tend to rise more quickly than large stocks during bull markets. But they're also usually more vulnerable to bear markets. During the week of the great crash of October 1987, for example, many small stocks lost 75 percent or more of their value, almost twice the catastrophic losses sustained by the blue chips.

INFLATION IS THE KEY

When are you most likely to win with small stocks? In this book, I've shown that inflation's impact on the economy is the single most important determinant of stock market trends. It's also the key to knowing when to buy small stocks.

Rising inflation is the death knell of bull markets in stocks. During a typical economic cycle, the economic train speeds up until it begins to overheat, bringing on inflation. The potential for ever-faster growth diminishes. Finally, the Fed, the conductor of our economic train, slams on the brakes by driving up interest rates. Economic growth screeches to a halt, and stocks plunge.

Like large stocks, small stocks also hit the skids when the Fed slows down the economic train. In fact, small stocks tend to be hit even harder than large ones during a market meltdown.

Rising inflation, particularly over a multiyear period, however, is unquestionably bullish for small stocks. Throughout the rampant inflation of the late 1970s and early 1980s, for example, small stocks outperformed large shares by a huge margin. And the same has been true of every other period where inflation was rising.

Why were small stocks able to run while the big boys stumbled? Because they have more growth potential and entail more risk than big stocks. They tend to do best when investors are focusing more on growth and less on risk.

When economic growth is running at its fastest, inflation is typically rising. So investors are very concerned with keeping up with inflation. Since small stocks' profits are steaming ahead much faster than those of the blue chips, growth companies are the shares of choice.

In contrast, during times of slow growth and moderate inflation, investors are more focused on safety. As a result, they opt for the slower but more reliable earnings growth of blue chip companies, like those listed in Chapter 10, and eschew the higher risks of growth stocks.

In addition, small stocks' earnings can grow much faster when inflation is high or rising than when it's low or falling. Since inflation is a key component of earnings, the higher it is, the faster growth can accelerate.

Faster inflation affects small companies' profits more than it does those of large firms because it causes less competitive market conditions, and less competition makes it easier for small firms to grow. When competition isn't intense, it's easier for a $1 million company to double its revenue than it is for a $100 million dollar company to do so.

By contrast, when inflation is falling, competition intensifies for ever-smaller markets. Big companies here tend to have the advantage. They can absorb economic shocks more easily. And they can reduce prices with less hardship to cut out competition. In contrast, a slow-growing economy makes it far more difficult for small companies to grow.

The table on page 142, "Inflation Is the Key," shows the proof of my thesis. It compares relative performances of the S&P 400 index and small stocks—as represented by the 20 percent of stocks with the lowest market capitalization—in different inflationary environments. Market capitalization is the price of a company's stock times its total number of shares traded. As such, it's an excellent point of compari-

INFLATION IS THE KEY

	Small Stocks	Large Stocks	Difference
Falling Inflation	8.4%	11.9%	−3.5%
Rising Inflation*	17.7	8.8	+8.9
Rising High Inflation†	21.2	9.4	+11.8
Rising Very High Inflation‡	26.2	9.6	+16.6

Average annual rates of return (5-year periods).
* Rising = 5-year consumer price index (CPI) average is above 10-year CPI average.
† High = 5-year CPI is greater than 5 percent.
‡ Very High = 5-year CPI is greater than 7 percent.

son for stocks' size. The higher the market capitalization, the bigger the company. Small stocks, in other words, have lower market capitalizations than larger ones.

For purposes of comparison, I have divided the period from 1933 to the present into five-year intervals, and averaged the results. Inflation is measured by the five and ten-year average rate of change in the Consumer Price Index (CPI). I consider inflation to be in a long-term downtrend whenever the five-year average annual rate of change in the CPI is below the ten-year average rate.

Whenever inflation has been in a downtrend, large stocks have outgained small stocks by an 11.9 percent to 8.4 percent margin. On the other hand, whenever inflation has been in an uptrend, small stocks have been the better performers. Under such conditions, small fry have surged an average of 17.7 percent. Large stocks, meanwhile, have returned only half as much, 8.8 percent.

The higher the most recent twelve-month inflation rate, the wider small stocks' margin of victory over the next twelve months, provided inflation is in a rising trend. When the twelve-month rate of increase in the CPI is greater than 5 percent, for example, small stocks have chalked up an average gain of 21.2 percent to big stocks' 9.4 percent. And finally, when inflation has been greater than 7 percent, the little guys have won by a margin of 26.2 percent to just 9.6 percent.

Small stocks' close relationship with inflation makes them a great inflation hedge. In fact, they're the best around—much better than gold.

Between 1976 and 1982, for example, inflation averaged 9 percent a year. Gold climbed from a low of $100 an ounce in 1976 to $450 an ounce in 1982. But small stocks during that same period climbed more than fivefold.

When inflation is high and rising, gold and other precious metals tend to return about 16 percent per year. That's far less than small stocks' average annual 21.2 percent gain.

THE 1-2 METHOD

Based on small stocks' relationship to inflation, I've developed two rules for investing in them. First, beef up your holdings of small stocks when you think inflation is going to rise over the next few years. Second, reduce your holdings, and beef up blue chip stakes, when you think inflation will fall.

If you follow these rules, you'll be way ahead of the pack in the long run. However, you can fine-tune your strategy by following my 1-2 method. It's based on two conditions.

Inflation must be in a long-term uptrend in order for small stocks to beat large ones. Consequently, condition 1 is for the five-year average annual rate of change in the CPI to be higher than the ten-year average annual rate of change.

Also, the higher the level of inflation at the start of the uptrend, the greater the outperformance of small stocks, relative to large ones. Condition 2, which is far less important, is for the five-year average annual rate of inflation (as represented by the CPI) to be above the historical average of 4.3 percent.

Suppose you were able to forecast whether inflation was going to rise or fall over the next five years. Then how would you have done by switching from large stocks to small stocks when inflation was rising and back again when inflation was falling? Since 1933, the average annual gain from following this strategy works out to nearly 17 percent.

Small stocks have outperformed big stocks by an average of 8.9 percent when condition 1 alone has been true. But when conditions 1 and 2 have been in force, small stocks' margin of victory has been 11.8 percent! In fact, they've never underperformed blue chips under those conditions.

When condition 1 has not been true, however, big stocks have almost always been tops. Their average margin of victory: 2.3 percent. Given small stocks' higher risk, almost anyone would have been far better off in bigger stocks.

Keep in mind that small stocks aren't immune to inflation-fueled bear markets. For example, if the economy is running on full—i.e., the conditions for a bear market are in force (rapidly falling unemployment claims, rising commodity prices, soaring or plummeting money supply growth, and low "real" interest rates—small stocks will probably fare even worse than big ones. Even if inflation is in a long-term rising trend, you don't want to own small stocks when a bear market is imminent.

But as long as inflation remains in a long-term uptrend, small stocks will outperform big ones mightily when the market recovers. So once stocks do hit bottom, you'll want to load up on small stocks, not big ones.

Small stocks also almost always outperform large stocks when one other condition is present: when the market is extremely overvalued, i.e., when P/Es are abnormally high (18 or higher).

As I explained in Chapter 6, high P/Es typically signal an explosion of economic growth. Overrapid growth almost always brings on inflation, which again benefits small stocks over large stocks.

Note that periods of overvaluation also typically lead to stock market meltdowns, during which small stocks often get hurt worse than large ones. But when inflation is high, small stocks almost always outperform the big boys during market rallies. As a result, as with periods of high inflation, when P/Es are abnormally high, small stocks are often the place to be.

PICKING HALF-PINTS

Like snowflakes, no two "half-pint" stocks are created equal. Some are headed for stardom. Some are destined for Wall Street's doghouse.

Back in the 1950s, for example, many of today's blue chips like IBM traded for scarcely a tenth of their current prices. Investors who bought then made out like bandits.

In hindsight, it seems as if it would have been a pretty simple decision to buy IBM. But in reality, only one in a thousand small companies will ever become a blue chip. And the winners are almost never the $2 and $3 stocks you hear about on a "hot tip."

Big stocks' larger size cushions them against disaster. In contrast, smaller companies are far more vulnerable to the effects of recessions, poor investments, competition, and lousy management. In fact, one false move by management, and the whole ship can go down.

Also, many promising small firms have been derailed by the unexpected death of a key board member. Large firms, in contrast, tend to be run by many people, with the ability to replace key personnel when needed.

In addition, small companies are often less well researched on Wall Street than larger ones. Unless you're careful, looming problems can go almost unnoticed until it's too late to get out.

Small growth stocks, particularly the very low-priced ones, tend to move on a dynamic of their own, often completely at odds with what's actually happening at the companies themselves. A broker's recommendation, or even a mention in a financial newsletter, can send them soaring or plummeting. And if you get caught in the way, the result can be deadly.

Then there's the problem of deciding when to sell a successful small stock pick. Some of the smartest people I know have blown big profits by trying to eke out a point or two more from a stock at its peak. Perhaps that's happened to you.

Back in mid-1987, at the height of a gold mania on Wall Street, a young friend of mine bought a small gold mining stock for $7 per share. He watched it rise to 13½. But then he got greedy, deciding to sell only if the stock reached $14. As it turned out, that never happened. And today the stock trades at barely 50 cents a share.

Others, anxious to lock in a profit, sell out too soon. My friend Al, for example, is still kicking himself for selling Intel at 20 back in 1989. (Since then it's broken 100!)

The biggest small-stock trap investors get snared in, however, is buying a stock with nothing behind it but great expectations. Losses can be especially egregious when the stocks have already had a great run.

I'll never forget one of my first clients, Edward. His brother-in-law, a broker, had convinced him to buy a little medical products company, which supposedly had developed a new drug that would provide treatment for all types of lung cancer. According to the broker, federal regulators were about to approve the drug for sale in the U.S. Edward also pointed out that the company had virtually no debt. Now he wanted my opinion on it.

After a little research, I discovered that the stock had already run up from 50 cents to $10 per share in just three months. True, the company had very little debt. But it also had no earnings. Sure, the stock had potential. But its steep run-up told me that investors were expecting the best already.

The company's entire fate rested on having its one drug meet the market's sky-high expectations. In other words, not only did it have to gain government approval quickly; after that, the drug had to be successfully marketed, while continuing to work flawlessly. If the company passed all of these critical tests, I reasoned, it could double again. But if it failed any of them, the stockholders could very easily get wiped out.

Edward, however, would hear none of my words of warning. Two days later, he bought 1,000 shares for $11 per share. For a little while, it seemed his gamble would pay off. Two weeks later, the stock hit a high of $13. But then came the news that the drug had an extremely harmful side effect, which would take months of research to remove. The company was able to borrow money to keep the project going. But the stock lost its luster in the eyes of investors. Two months later, it touched a low of just $2 per share.

Edward, as it turned out, had the good sense to sell out at $6. He had lost a bit of money. But he learned a valuable lesson: When you shop for growth stocks, don't buy on a promise; stick with quality. Since then, he's been quite successful.

Surprisingly few small stock investors shop for quality. That's why small fry are one of the biggest graveyards for the capital of the unwary, second only to penny stocks and partnerships. Unless you're willing to spend time thoroughly researching your stock picks, you're better off buying growth stocks through a mutual fund.

But if you're willing to do a bit of research to seek out quality, you'll almost certainly have your share of future IBMs and Xeroxes. And, even if inflation does remain in a long-term downtrend, you'll beat the market. In contrast, most small stock mutual funds will lag well behind big stocks in times of low inflation.

RECOGNIZING QUALITY

Quality is the key to buying the best growth stocks. The surest way to reap the biggest profits and avoid the pitfalls is to buy quality growth stocks and hold them, unless they no longer qualify as quality shares.

Our criteria for quality are described in detail below. Quality small shares should meet all of them. One easy place to get data on all of these items is *Value Line Investment Survey*, which can be found in most libraries. If a company is not listed there, the best idea is to get its latest annual report:

- *Rising earnings growth for at least ten years, or for as long as the stock has been publicly traded.* Rising earnings are what propels a growth stock upward. Stocks with little or no earnings are an unknown quantity. They could turn out to be wildly profitable if their promise translates into rising profits. But there's nothing to cushion their fall if those expectations turn out to be empty. Generally, the best stocks are those with long-term (at least five-year) profit growth rates of at least 10 percent.

  To find a company's earnings growth rate, divide profits per share for the current year by those of the previous year. For example, if the company earns $2 per share in 1993 and $1.50 per share in 1992, the annual earnings growth rate is 33 percent ($2 ÷ $1.50 = 1.33, or 33 percent).

- *Rock-solid balance sheet.* The best measure of a firm's financial health is its debt-to-equity ratio (long-term debt divided by share-holders' equity). Specifically, long-term debt must be less than one-half of stockholders' equity. Low debt means the company will be able to cut costs during economic downturns. In contrast, high debt firms can be forced to curtail expansion plans dramatically should sales growth slow unexpectedly.

NEW HORIZONS, DEAD ENDS

Many Wall Street pros use a relative P/E ratio to determine whether small or large stocks are the better buy. For large stocks, they use the S&P 400 average. For small fry, they look at the T. Rowe Price New Horizons mutual fund, one of the nation's first small stock funds.

Specifically, they divide New Horizons' average P/E by the S&P 400 P/E to find the "relative" P/E for growth stocks. For example, if both New Horizons and the S&P 400 trade at a P/E of 20, the relative P/E is 1 (20 ÷ 20).

As I pointed out in Chapter 6, the higher a stock's P/E, the more the market generally expects the company's earnings to rise. Therefore, because of their greater growth potential, small stocks tend to have higher P/Es than blue chips. As a result, the New Horizons fund has almost always had a higher P/E than the S&P 400 average.

Historically, the relative P/E has ranged between 2—where New Horizons' P/E is twice that of the S&P 400—and 1 where the P/Es of both are roughly equal. When the relative P/E is on the high end of the range, blue chips are considered a better value. When the relative P/E is on the low end, small stocks are favored.

Taking this one step further, many analysts advocate buying small stocks when the relative P/E is hovering around 1, and loading up on blue chips when it hits close to 2.

This strategy, however, is full of holes. First, the New Horizons fund has only been around since January 1969. This period has included both ups and downs for small stocks. But it's a relatively short period of time on which to build conclusions.

Second, New Horizons contains only a small percentage of the total universe of small stocks. Consequently, there are no guarantees that it provides a representative sample.

Most important, relative P/Es at best can only tell us when small stocks are relatively cheap. They do a remarkably poor job of telling us when small stocks will outperform big ones, and vice versa.

Relative P/Es fail to be good market-timing indicators for the same reason that P/Es do: They don't take inflation into account. Similarly, the relative P/Es of small and large stocks are useful for market timing only when put into the context of inflation. Otherwise, they're meaningless.

- *Free Cash Flow*. The company should have money left over after paying all of its expenses, including interest on loans and construction costs. This money is called free cash flow. It can be used for stock repurchases, dividend boosts, to expand or buy out other companies, or simply to beef up the company's investments. In all cases, shareholders benefit.
- *Rising operating margins that are within a percentage point or two of all-time highs*. This is gross profit from a company's operations, the best measure of how profitable a company is. A rising margin indicates that the company has secured a profitable niche market in which its dominance will produce big profits in the years ahead. It's calculated by dividing a company's total revenue by total operating expenses (excluding debt payments).
- *Relatively low P/E ratio*. A stock with high growth potential and a low P/E is a rare find indeed. Specifically, we want companies whose P/Es are no more than twice the five-year profit growth rate. In other words, if a company has a five-year profit growth rate of 10 percent, and a P/E of 30, it's not acceptable. But if its earnings growth rate were 20 percent, it would be.

Stocks that meet these criteria stand the best chance of becoming tomorrow's blue chips. If you buy them now, you'll have a chance to double, triple, and quintuple your money, simply by buying and holding, even if the long-term trend in inflation stays down in the 1990s and small stocks trail the blue chips. You'll do even better if inflation rears its ugly head.

Of course, not every firm that meets these criteria will find its way to the top of the heap. So, no matter how good a certain small stock may look now, you'll have to keep careful tabs on its progress to make sure it continues to meet my criteria.

One further point: you'll dramatically increase the odds of your success in small stocks if you own at least 6 or 7 different stocks. Perhaps even more so than with blue chips, small stocks' performance can be shattered by a chance event, such as the death or retirement of a key employee or a lawsuit.

The only real way to guard against potential catastrophes is to diversify. Those who don't want to shell out for that many stocks are better off choosing a top-notch mutual fund, the subject of our next chapter.

POINTS TO REMEMBER

1. Small stocks have more profit potential and greater risk than large stocks, because they have more room to grow.
2. Small stocks as a group are a better investment than larger stocks when P/Es are abnormally high and when inflation is in a long-term uptrend. These two conditions often occur at the same time.
3. Focus on small stocks when inflation is in a long-term uptrend, or when explosive economic growth (rapid inflation) is expected. Otherwise, stick with large stocks.
4. To find great small stocks, use the same criteria for picking great big stocks: dominance in an emerging market, consistent earnings growth, and solid finances.

12

Seven Steps to Mutual Fund Profits

I FIRMLY BELIEVE THAT BUYING INDIVIDUAL QUALITY STOCKS is the best way to profit from my market-timing models. The best stocks will outperform the market dramatically in good markets. And they'll mostly hold their own when stocks fall.

It's absolutely essential, however, that you own shares in at least seven or eight different companies at the same time. Otherwise, you could be wiped out by an unexpected disaster at one of the companies. No matter how careful you've been to pick a dominant company with a strong financial history—and even if the market is blasting out to new highs—you can still lose your shirt if you overcommit to a single stock. Unfortunately, most investors learn that lesson the hard way.

In the early 1980s, for example, IBM was by far the dominant producer of computer technology, one of the real growth technologies of the future. The company's profit margins were at record levels and had been rising for some time. Finances were impeccable. The company's five-year earnings growth rate was well into double digits. And the stock had been a leader in the 1983–84 bull market rally. In short, IBM was the premier growth stock in America, and showed every sign of continuing to be for years to come.

Just eight years later, however, all that had changed. IBM's earnings had fallen to less than half the levels of the early 1980s. Margins were squeezed, and the stock was actually at a lower level than in 1984. The reason: The company's management had realized too late that personal computers were replacing the mainframe units that were its bread and butter.

By the early 1990s, the upsurge in competition still hadn't ended

IBM's industry dominance. In fact, the company still has great promise. But the years of easy growth are over.

The point is that any one stock, no matter how good it looks, can take a bath. For example, if your entire portfolio had been in IBM for the past eight years, you would have missed the entire bull market of the 1980s. Things happen.

Of course, for those who owned IBM as only a small part of their portfolios, Big Blue was only a minimal drag on their returns, which brings me to my main point. No matter how good a market timer you are, maintaining a diversified portfolio is vital to stock market success. Any stock, no matter how good it looks on paper, can take a dive if circumstances are right.

THE FEELING IS MUTUAL

Most portfolios can easily handle the expense of owning shares in seven or eight individual companies. But some investors' portfolios are simply too small.

Moreover, most individual shares must be purchased through a broker. So, commission expenses can be steep for smaller players who can't afford to buy a round lot (100 shares). Owning individual shares also means you've got to keep a close watch on your holdings, to be sure finances are still strong and that the firm's dominant market position is still intact. Some people just don't have the time to spare.

That's where mutual funds—professionally managed pools that hold portfolios of many stocks—come in. At their best, funds provide you with a share of a portfolio of great stocks, at a fraction of the cost of doing it in the market. You can buy and sell them at no cost. And you can leave the choice of holdings up to the fund manager, freeing up your time for other things.

Mutual funds can be especially helpful for young savers who are just beginning to build up their portfolios. Many funds allow shareholders to invest as little as $100 at a time.

Of course, mutual fund gains are almost never as great as those from individual stocks. The reason is simple. Funds manage millions of dollars, so even the best ones almost always wind up overdiversifying, i.e., owning too many shares. The laggard stocks will bring down the performance of the overall portfolio.

But for many investors, especially those early savers, any sacrifice of potential gains is well worth the advantages that funds offer. And once your holdings are built up, you can then begin to cash in on the big gain potential of individual stocks.

In the past twenty years or so, mutual funds have gone from relative obscurity to America's investment of choice. There are now funds available for almost any taste or specialty, whether it be growth stocks, municipal bonds, or gold. And there are many great funds out there managed by real professionals, which beat the market every year.

But mutual fund investing is certainly no free lunch. In fact, the overwhelming majority of funds underperform the market every year. And just as a bad portfolio of stocks can derail the most carefully planned market-timing strategy, so can a lousy mutual fund. Worse, many funds eat you alive with fees, sales loads, and hidden expense charges.

The biggest offenders on both of these scores tend to be broker-sponsored funds. These are pushed by full-service brokers onto the firm's clients. The broker takes a big commission and the investor is left holding the bag of rising expenses and mediocre performance.

It's truly amazing how many people are unaware of these pitfalls. That's why it's just as essential to pick the right mutual funds as it is to pick the right stocks. To this end, I've devised a seven-step system for picking the best mutual funds. There's nothing fancy about either my system or the funds it pinpoints. These funds are simply those best suited for our market-timing strategy. They may not always be the market's best performers each quarter or even each year. But over the long haul, if you use them in conjunction with my market timing system, you'll regularly beat the Wall Street pros.

Rule 1: Always Buy Funds with No Sales Charges or "Loads." Never Buy a "Loaded" Mutual Fund.

A sales charge, or load, is a fee some mutual funds assess against any new investment. Funds use these loads to cover their marketing costs.

For example, if a fund charges a 4 percent sales load, a new $1,000 investment would be assessed $40. Consequently, a new investor's stake will be down to $960, from the $1,000 they originally put up.

It doesn't take an M.B.A. from Harvard to figure out that the more money you have going to work for you on the front end, the more you stand to make. Our theoretical new investor, for example, will have to make almost 5 percent on his money just to break even. In contrast, with no-load funds, fully 100 percent of your money goes to work for you right away.

Some loaded funds try to justify their high prices by touting supposedly superior performance. But I've found that there's almost always a no-load fund that's done just as well, if not better. And once you figure in the fees, there's no comparison.

Don't let anyone kid you. No-load funds are always best.

Rule 2: Avoid Funds That Charge Exit Fees, or "Back-end" Loads.

Some funds claim to be no-load because they don't charge a fee to new shareholders. But for those who want to cash out, they assess hefty exit fees.

This sneaky strategy can be a powerful disincentive to keep you from acting on crucial market-timing signals. Avoid these funds.

Rule 3: Check the Fund's Performance in Bear as Well as Bull Markets. Make Sure That, on Average, It Consistently Beat the S&P 400 Index.

A rising tide raises all ships. That's why almost any fund does well during a bull market. The key question, however, is did the fund beat the market averages. In my comparisons, I always use the S&P 400 index, just as I use it to size up all of the indicators in this book.

Specifically, I look for funds that have beaten the S&P 400 stock index average consistently over the last three years. Managers of these funds have shown they have the knack for picking good stocks over a multiyear period.

If you choose only funds that meet this criterion, you probably still won't do as well as you would by picking individual quality shares.

But as long as you adhere to my market-timing rules, your profits will be generous.

Superior bull market performance, however, is not enough. Suppose, for example, that you bought a fund at a major crisis point (see Chapter 9) that our system does not alert you to, and it falls precipitously during the bear market that follows. If the fund is a poor bear market performer, it could get especially hammered. So, it could take years for you to recoup your losses, let alone realize the fund's superior long-term returns.

That's why I look for funds that have also done well in bear markets. As I write this, the two most recent bear market periods for most stocks are the last six months of 1990 and the last six months of 1987. Specifically, I look for funds that have beaten the S&P on average during both of those periods.

Funds that beat the market during both bull and bear markets won't guarantee you big profits. But if you use them in conjunction with the market-timing strategy I've laid down here, odds are great that you'll be making many happy trips to the bank.

Rule 4: Gauge the Fund's Risk by Checking Its Portfolio for Diversification and Volatility.

The phrase "past performance is no guarantee of future results" is a well-worn cliche on Wall Street. Unfortunately, many investors that have chased the "hot" funds of the moment have found it to be true over and over again.

Most vulnerable to this pitfall are funds that have overweighted—placed a large percentage of their assets—into a particular stock or stock group. This leaves them open to the same types of problems that can affect the owner of an undiversified stock portfolio. An unforeseen incident such as a surprise lawsuit, the death of a key director, the passage of new federal legislation, or a hundred other factors can bring down the whole show.

One very well known and highly successful fund manager I know, for example, heavily commited his fund to up-and-coming growth stock Home Shopping Network several years ago. Since then, the company's hot streak has cooled off a bit, and the stock has fallen by almost 40 percent from its highs. My friend's fund has struggled ever since.

Also at risk are the numerous "sector" funds now available, which specialize in a particular industry group. The most successful of these in recent years have been health-care funds. The aging of America has created a large demand for medical research, products, and services. These funds buy shares in the companies that are meeting that demand.

Unfortunately these stocks are also very popular. Consequently, they're very expensive and vulnerable to bear markets. In the early months of 1992, for example, formerly high-flying biotechnology stocks were actually among the worst-performing stock groups.

How can you avoid funds that are overly committed to a few stocks? I use two tests: the fund's standard deviation of returns, and r squared, which measures how closely a fund mirrors the market. The higher a fund's r squared, the more closely it mirrors the market, the more diversified it is, and the less vulnerable it is to disaster in a single stock. Generally r squareds of 70 or higher are diversified enough.

Standard deviation looks at a fund's volatility. The lower the standard deviation, the less the risk. Anything with a standard deviation greater than the S&P 400 has less volatile returns than the market.

Standard deviation and r squared aren't perfect gauges. And sometimes a fund's performance is so good I can't resist recommending it, even if it is more volatile and less diversified than I'd normally like it to be. But funds that meet these standards are less risky, and hence generally better vehicles for implementing my market-timing strategy.

Rather than trying to calculate standard deviation and r squared on your own, I would advise consulting one of the numerous sources that report them. The most complete source I've found is Chicago-based *Morningstar Mutual Funds* (subscription information is available by calling 800-876-5005). It's found in many libraries. Some funds can also provide you with this information, but you'll have to be persistent.

Rule 5: Make Sure the Fund's Track Record Is Also That of the Current Manager.

A fund's success or failure depends almost entirely on the skill of its manager or managers. Only if the manager is adept at both picking great stocks and timing the market will the fund be able to beat the market year after year.

As a result, choosing great mutual funds means picking the best managers. The best fund managers are, by definition, those with the best performance. So, logically, the easiest way to choose funds with the best managers is to pick the funds with the best records beating the market.

Unfortunately, it's not that easy. A fund's manager can change at the drop of a hat. As with any other business, mutual fund companies compete with each other to land the best managers. Just as in baseball or basketball, a highly sought-after star who commands a premium price can leave a fund to take a better job at another fund. Also, many managers who have had successful careers choose to retire to enjoy the finer things in life.

If you're a shareholder of a fund that's lost a successful manager, there's no guarantee that the next manager will be able to match the last one's performance. Every manager has his or her own style and penchant for risk, which may not match those of the prior manager.

Perhaps the biggest shock to mutual fund investors in recent years came back in May 1990. That's when the legendary Peter Lynch dropped a bombshell on the investment world by retiring as manager of growth mutual fund Fidelity Magellan to spend more time with his family.

During his thirteen-year career, Lynch had compiled an average annual gain of 29.1 percent for the fund, nearly twice the S&P 500's 15.8 percent gain. Under his direction, Magellan grew to become the largest fund in America. But despite the fund's great size, Lynch had consistently been able to pinpoint bargains and remain ahead of the pack, generating great returns.

Lynch's departure sent a shock wave through the investment community. But fortunately for Magellan and its shareholders, his successor, Morris Smith, proved up to the task of managing the fund. His average annual return of 14.7 percent beat the S&P 500's 9.8 percent gain.

Though that record was not as impressive as Lynch's, it was still good enough to attract 54 percent more money to the fund. But less than two years later, Smith announced his own retirement from the megafund, leaving investors pondering whether or not his successor would be up to the task.

And this story is not unique. Scores of funds change managers every year. In fact, with very few exceptions, it's likely that most successful fund managers will leave their funds over the next few years.

The lesson: Keep tabs on your fund to be aware of any change in management. If there is a change, don't necessarily exit the fund. But check out the new manager's track record at his or her old fund. Then compare the old fund to the new fund and decide if you think the manager will be able to perform just as well at your fund. If the answer is yes, hold on. But before sinking more money into the fund, wait a couple of quarters to be sure.

Alternatively, you can stick to funds that are managed by a group of advisers. These funds are governed more by a set strategy and philosophy, rather than the instincts and skills of a single manager. As a result, a change in personnel, no matter how talented they are, probably won't have nearly as profound an effect on their performance as it would on a one-man show.

Rule 6: Check Your Fund's Prospectus to Guard Against Hidden Fees.

Almost all mutual funds bill their shareholders for such expenses as managers' salaries, market research, and transaction fees. Many funds also bill shareholders for the cost of marketing the fund to new investors. These expenses are named 12b-1 fees, after an SEC rule by that name.

You can't avoid these fees entirely. But you can avoid funds with the most outrageous costs. Funds must publish a schedule of all fees, as a percentage of assets, in their prospectuses.

Generally, the higher the percentage of assets paid in fees, the worse the fund. But what's high and what's low can vary greatly, depending on the type of fund. Funds that trade stocks frequently to time the market, for example, will incur much higher expenses than will funds that do virtually no trading. But their performance may be sufficiently superior to justify it.

As a rule of thumb, stock funds should have total annual expenses (management and marketing fees) of no more than 1.5 percent, and preferably no more than one percent. Funds with expenses in the 2 percent range should be avoided. Never buy a bond fund with expenses of more than 1 percent.

Another point: Check your fund's turnover regularly. It, too, is published in the prospectus. With most no-load funds, you can trade in and out as frequently as you want. You can buy when the indicators say buy, and sell when they say sell. Funds that do a lot of trading may be 90 percent cash at market bottoms. So if you buy them expecting to get a play on stocks, you could be sadly disappointed. Only with funds that hold a relatively constant portfolio will you be assured of profiting from stocks' rebound.

Turnover is measured as a percentage of the total portfolio. The higher the turnover, the more frequently the fund's assets are traded. For example, if a fund has $1 billion in assets and trades $200 million worth of stock in a given year, its turnover is 20 percent ([$200 million ÷ $1 billion] × 100). Generally, turnover of more than 150 percent for most funds could indicate excessive trading. Watch your step.

Rule 7: Know Your Fund's Family.

In the classic movie *The Godfather,* Don Corleone lectures his son Michael on the importance of family. But if he were advising him on mutual funds, he would emphasize the same thing, family.

A fund family is basically a group of mutual funds organized and marketed by the same institution. It's extremely important for several reasons.

First, if there is a change in management, the most likely successors are managers of the family's other funds. Both of Fidelity Magellan's managers after Peter Lynch, for example, came from other Fidelity funds. Fidelity also follows a practice of alternating its sector fund managers every few years.

Second, switching accounts between mutual funds of different families can take days or weeks. And that time can mean big money. Switching money between funds in the same family, however, can be done almost immediately with a simple phone call, and most often at no charge.

That's why the choice of funds offered by a family is so crucial. To use my market-timing strategy, any funds you choose should feature, at a minimum, at least one great stock fund to switch into when the signals are bullish, and a money market fund to move into when the signals turn bearish.

POINTS TO REMEMBER

1. Mutual funds are not as profitable [do not offer as much potential return] as stocks of great companies. But if you can't afford to build a balanced portfolio of shares in at least seven or eight companies, you can make big money if you pick only the best funds.
2. The best way to pick the best funds is to follow the seven steps outlined in this chapter:
   (a) Always buy funds with no sales charges or "loads." Never buy a "loaded" mutual fund.
   (b) Avoid funds that charge exit fees, or "back-end" loads.
   (c) Check the fund's performance in bear as well as bull markets. Make sure that, on average, it consistently beat the S&P 400 index.
   (d) Gauge the fund's risk by checking its portfolio for diversification and volatility.
   (e) Make sure the fund's track record is also that of the current manager.
   (f) Check your fund's prospectus to guard against hidden fees.
   (g) Know your fund's family.

13

Economic Forecasting

By NOW YOU SHOULD BE ABLE to see why you don't have to forecast economic growth in order to predict stock market trends. And now that you understand the concepts of my market system, I've got a surprise. You can use the indicators in this book to predict the economy—and with considerable accuracy. This in turn will enable you to predict market trends even more effectively.

Economic and market-timing indicators are interchangeable precisely because the market's moves are one of the key indicators of economic trends. The reason? Stock prices have little or nothing to do with what's going on in the economy now. Rather, they're based on investors' expectations of companies' future earnings. The higher profits are expected to go, the more investors will pay for shares of stock.

Corporate profits rise in good times and fall in bad. Therefore, stock prices typically rise when good times are in the offing and fall when bad times lie ahead.

One of the best examples of the stock market's powerful ability to forecast economic trends was its collosal run-up from early 1991 to mid-1992. As I point out in Chapter 9, 1991 dawned with Saddam Hussein's army entrenched in Kuwait and posing a clear threat to the world's oil supply. Oil prices were skyrocketing. Meanwhile, the U.S. economy was sliding into its first recession since the early 1980s. Unemployment began to soar. As for stocks, the Dow had anticipated the economic slowdown by nosediving from almost 3000 to the 2300 area.

Then came Operation Desert Storm and the subsequent defeat of the Iraqi troops. Oil prices plummeted. Recognizing that the economic threat was over, stocks were off to the races. The S&P went on to rise 30 percent during the next twelve months.

The stock market's fabulous rally projected something that few on either Wall Street or Main Street saw at that time: The economy was about to boom. The media pundits and million-dollar economists continued to whine about a coming economic collapse. But the stock market was sending a loud and clear message that a powerful economic recovery was in the making.

After the first quarter of 1991, growth in the U.S. economy began to pick up steam. And by early 1992, the annual growth rate of our Gross Domestic Product (a measure of the total value of all goods and services produced in the country) was approaching 3 percent and heading much higher.

Admittedly, the stock market can't predict the strength of a recovery or the depth of a recession; it can only give a general idea of what lies ahead. Also, there's often a time lag involved.

One example of off-timing was the lag between stocks' explosive rally early in 1991 and the economy's burst of growth in mid-1992. The reason for this relatively long lag period is easily understandable: The recession of 1990–91 was comparatively mild.

Even during that recession's worst days, the economic statistics were not nearly as bad as they had been in prior slowdowns, such as the early 1980s. Because they had less room for improvement, most key economic indicators improved at a far slower rate than they had in previous recoveries, when the economy had a long way to climb.

The slow rate of improvement was misinterpreted as a sign of further weakness ahead. That was a major reason why economists took so long to realize that a recovery indeed was in progress. It wasn't that the stock market had proved to be a poor forecaster. Rather, it was the economists who misinterpreted signs of a recovery.

MY SYSTEM

Stocks' close relationship to economic trends means we can use an adjusted version of our model to forecast economic trends with considerable accuracy. In fact, stocks can provide some of the most devastatingly accurate predictions of economic trends around.

The system I profile here will put you light years ahead of most so-called economics experts in terms of forecasting what lies ahead for economic growth. It can give you a leg up on the competition in your business and profession, no matter what path of life you're on. And it can improve your stock market timing even more.

The key to any economic forecast is price-to-earnings ratios. As I discussed in Chapter 6, P/Es are the best gauge of how the market values a particular stock or the stock market in general.

To review, the higher a stock's P/E, the more investors are willing to pay for each dollar of the company's latest earnings per share. Investors are willing to pay more or less for a dollar of profits, depending on how much or how little they expect those profits to rise in the future.

Consequently, stocks have above-average P/Es when investors' expectations about their profit growth are high. The higher the P/E, the greater are investors' expectations. In other words, P/Es are the best measure of what the stock market is forecasting for earnings and hence the economy.

How good a predictor of economic growth are P/Es? P/Es coincide with moves in my other key indicators: high P/Es tend to precede big drops in unemployment insurance claims, which are a sign of an impending stock market top.

The table "P/Es and Changes in Commodity Prices" shows how well P/Es have tended to forecast moves in another of my key indicators—commodity prices. Like anything else, commodities tend to rise in price as demand for them rises. Since they're the building blocks of everything else in the economy, commodities are in rising demand when economic growth is picking up steam. Consequently, rising commodity prices are a sign of escalating economic growth and another sign of an impending stock market top.

As you can see, during the twelve months following a time when the average P/E of the S&P 400 has been greater than 18, commodity prices have risen an average of 8 percent. That level is typical of huge upswings in economic growth and is also very bearish for stocks.

However, when the S&P 400 has an average P/E of less than 12, commodity prices have risen an anemic 1.2 percent on average. Such stunted hikes in commodity prices are typical during recessions. And

P/ES AND CHANGES IN COMMODITY PRICES

Average P/E of S&P 400	12-Month Change In Commodity Prices
Greater than 18	+8.0%
15 to 18	+3.2
12 to 15	+0.2
Less than 12	1.2

this is another sign of how low P/Es, i.e., low investor expectations about corporate profits, anticipate subpar economic growth.

The relationship of P/Es to economic growth becomes even more striking when you compare various levels of P/Es with "coincident indicators." Coincident indicators measure economic growth that's going on right now; so they're real-time indicators.

In contrast, changes in leading indicators tend to occur before changes in economic growth; changes in lagging indicators tend to occur after changes in economic growth.

To find out how the economy is doing right now, I use the Commerce Department's index of coincident indicators, released monthly. There are four coincident indicators:

- *Personal income* (an estimate of all the money made by working Americans over a particular period). A growing economy means more jobs are created, and ultimately this leads to higher wages and salaries. Both of these things increase personal income, which reflects the current level of economic growth.
- *Manufacturing sales* (how much businesses are buying). Since businesses by definition buy more when the economy is growing ever faster, manufacturing sales also very much reflect the trend in economic growth.
- *Payroll employment* (number of people on payrolls). This has little predictive value as far as stocks are concerned. But because it roughly reflects how many people are employed at a certain time, it's an excellent indication of how the economy is doing.
- *Industrial production* (the total output of American factories, utilities, and mines). Activity in each of these areas rises sharply when the economy picks up steam.

Taken together, these four indicators present the most accurate picture available of where the economy stands at any given moment. To make things more convenient, the Commerce Department averages their twelve-month rates of growth into a single figure. The higher the result, the faster the economy is growing at that moment.

For example, say personal income has grown 3 percent over the latest twelve-month period. At the same time, manufacturing sales are up 4 percent, payroll employment has increased 6 percent, and industrial production is up 2 percent. The current average rate of increase in these indicators would then be 3.75 percent. From that, the Commerce Department comes up with a final figure that shows the economy's twelve-month rate of growth to be 3.75 percent as well.

The chart below compares the average twelve-month change in the coincident indicator average with various levels of P/Es.

After the average P/E on the S&P 400 moves above 18, economic growth as measured by the coincident indicators has been 5.4 percent during the following twelve months, which is quite robust. In other words, when the S&P 400's P/E rises to 19 or higher, a point where investors' expectations for stocks and corporate earnings are at a peak, an extremely powerful surge in economic growth has almost always resulted.

In contrast, when average P/Es have been low (less than 12) economic growth as measured by the coincident indicators has been only 0.8 percent on average during the next twelve months. Again, this result is just what you'd expect. Low P/Es, i.e., low investor expecta-

CHANGE IN COINCIDENT INDICATORS

P/E of S&P 400	Change in Economic Indicators 12 Months Forward
Greater than 18	+5.4%
15 to 18	+1.5
12 to 15	+1.1
Less than 12	+0.8

NOTE: 12 out of 18 times with P/Es less than 8.5, the coincident indicators declined in the following 12 months.

tions for corporate earnings growth and stocks, typically precede slow economic growth.

P/Es in the 12 to 18 range have usually coincided with moderate economic growth. This too makes sense. Moderate profit growth expectations are normally a sign that moderate economic growth lies ahead. (Note that for all P/E calculations I've used cash-flow adjusted earnings as I did in Chapter 6. This factors out any abnormalities caused by one-time fluctuations in reported profits.)

A MODEL THAT WORKS

As I've shown, P/Es alone can give you a pretty good idea of where the economy is headed. Following their cues about growth will enable you to forecast the economy better than 99 percent of the million-dollar economists who fritter away their time watching obscure statistics like new home sales and making dull speeches.

You can, however, sharpen your economic forecast even further by adding in a few more indicators, shown in our formula below. This model contains many of the same indicators that I used to forecast the stock market.

−16.3
− (0.17 × the percentage change in commodity prices over the past four months)
+ (0.06 × the 12-month percentage growth in the M2 money supply)
+ (0.05 × the S&P 400 12-month gain)
+ (0.35 × the current P/E of the S&P 400 [based on cash flow earnings, see Chap. 6])
+ (5.88 × the ratio of AAA bond yield to T-bill yields)
+ (0.81 × the rate of change in the government's index of leading economic indicators for the last four months)
+ (0.23 × earnings growth for the S&P 400 over the last 12 months)

= Projected 12-month percentage change in the coincident indicators

The reason for the overlap in my economic and stock market models is simple. My indicators are all designed to measure the economy's potential for sustainable economic growth. The stock market only performs well when the economic train has a lot of room to increase its speed without igniting inflation. A speeding train has nothing to do but slow down or jump the track. Either scenario means slowing growth ahead, a negative for stocks and the economy.

For a review of what each indicator means, see the appropriate chapters: commodity prices (Chapter 2), money supply growth (Chapter 5), P/Es (Chapter 6), and the AAA bond/T-bill yield ratio (Chapter 4). Note that I use the M2 measure of the money supply this time because it corresponds better to economic trends.

There are also two indicators included that aren't discussed in earlier chapters:

1. The stock market's (S&P 400) twelve-month average gain. The concept behind this is simple: The more the stock market has risen over the past twelve months, the better the economy has tended to perform. That's because, as I explained above, bull markets in stocks tend to predict strong economic growth. This, you'll recall, is also the same principle behind Unexpected Gains (see Chapter 8).

2. Four-month rate of change in the Commerce Department's index of leading economic indicators. This is a compilation of several economic indicators that are commonly used on Wall Street to predict economic trends. It's calculated monthly, with revisions the following month, and it's found on page C-1 of the *Survey of Current Business*.

The index has had a modest record of forecasting general market trends. For example, three months of consecutive declines by the index have almost never failed to forecast a recession.

On its own, the index's frequent revisions dramatically diminish its effectiveness as a forecaster. Also, it's of little use in projecting the absolute level of economic growth that lies ahead. But it does sum up a number of indicators that our model does not include. And it includes several indicators, such as unemployment insurance claims, that are part of our stock market model. Consequently, it adds a bit more predictive power to our model.

Note that two of the indicators in my model carry a good deal more weight than the others: P/Es and the AAA bond/T-bill yield spread. P/Es are very important because they are the only indicator that shows what the stock market is forecasting for the economy. As I noted earlier, the stock market is by far the most effective economic indicator on its own. Note that here I'm talking about unadjusted P/Es, rather than the inflation-adjusted, or "real," P/Es I use in my stock market forecasting model.

As I pointed out in Chapter 4, the AAA-rated corporate bond/ Treasury bill yield ratio is very important because it reflects the inflation component in interest rates. The greater the ratio, the larger the real growth component.

When businesses expect economic growth to be relatively high, they're willing to pay higher rates of interest in order to borrow money. Long-term interest rates are represented by yields on twenty-year AAA corporate bonds and short-term rates by 3-month Treasury bill yields. The higher longer-term rates are, the more businesses are willing to pay to borrow to finance future growth. Businesses are willing to pay higher rates only if they expect big returns.

For example, suppose AAA-rated bonds are yielding 6 percent and T-bills are yielding 4 percent. Businesses are expecting less growth than they would be if AAA bonds were yielding 8 percent and T-bills yielding 3 percent.

Like the stock market, businesses' willingness to borrow tends to be an excellent indicator of future economic growth. That's why the AAA-rated corporate bond/T-bill yield ratio is such an important part of my economic forecasting model.

Now let's look at how the model works together. Suppose commodity prices have risen 6 percent during the last four months. At the same time, the twelve-month rate of growth in M2 is 2 percent, the stock market has risen 10 percent in the last twelve months, cash-flow-adjusted P/Es are 18, the AAA bond/T-bill yield ratio is 2, the rate of change in the index of leading indicators is 2 percent for the last 4 months, and the earnings of the S&P 400 have grown 5 percent during the past twelve months.

Note that I use a four-month period for commodity prices. The reason is that these indicators better reflect current economic trends.

The longer periods are better stock market forecasters. The model below shows how to calculate the result:

$$
\begin{array}{l}
-\ 16.3 \\
-\ 1.02\ (0.17 \times 6) \\
+\ 0.12\ (0.06 \times 2) \\
+\ 0.5\ (0.05 \times 10) \\
+\ 6.3\ (0.35 \times 18) \\
+\ 11.76\ (5.88 \times 2) \\
+\ 1.62\ (0.81 \times 2) \\
+\ 1.15\ (0.23 \times 5) \\
\hline
\end{array}
$$

= 4.13 percent change in the coincident indicators during the next 12 months

In other words, under the conditions I've just described above, the coincident indicators should rise 4.13 percent over the next twelve months. That's pretty rapid growth, the kind that might cause an overvalued market to stumble.

Note that all the indicators are positively related to economic growth except commodity prices. These are all inversely related to economic growth. The higher they are, the less the projected growth rate will be. The higher the others are, the faster the economy should grow.

A MODEL PERFORMANCE

How have my model's projections measured up as an economic forecaster? The table on page 170 shows the results since World War II. The record is by no means perfect. But it's accurate enough to plan your life (or business) around with a great degree of confidence.

For example, whenever projected rates of growth in the coincident indicators have been at least 4 percent, actual economic growth has averaged a rapid 5.8 percent during the next twelve months. Projections below −2 percent have, true to form, presaged a shrinking economy—economic growth has been a negative 5 percent over the

PROJECTED VS. ACTUAL CHANGE IN COINCIDENT INDICATORS

Projected Growth According to My Model	Average Actual Change in Coincident Indicators for the Next 12 Months
Less than −4	−5.2
−2 to −4	−5.0
0 to −2	−1.3
0 to +2	+0.9
2 to 4	+4.7
4 to 6	+5.8
Greater than 6	+7.7

In all 23 instances in which the model was less than −4, the economy contracted over the next 12 months. In 76 out of 77 cases in which the model projected growth of 4 to 6 percent, the economy grew over the next 12 months. It grew all 104 times the model was greater than 6.

next twelve months. The bottom line: This model gives the most consistently accurate economic forecasts I know of.

Accurately forecasting the economy can be very important in running your life. Should you make that big purchase of a car or house now? Or will interest rates come down over the next year, easing your way? Is it worth the risk of switching jobs now? The answer you get from the simple calculation above can go a long way toward answering those questions.

Most central to this book, however, is how economic forecasting relates to investing. And that's where it really gets interesting. In fact, these economic forecasts can actually project changes in my stock market forecasting system.

Bullish projections about the economy are often warning signs that our projections for stocks are about to turn negative. Conversely, bearish projections can mean that a buying opportunity is close at hand.

Remember, the market runs on empty; it dies on full. The faster the economic train moves, the less it can increase its speed. Sooner or later, it will have to slow down, or at least stop speeding up. Either way, stocks' glory days will be over.

When the economy is booming, all your friends will probably be falling all over themselves to buy stocks. And that's precisely when you want to be heading for the exits.

POINTS TO REMEMBER

1. Many of the same indicators I use to forecast the market can also be used to predict the economy's rate of growth with considerable accuracy.
2. I use the Commerce Department's index of coincident indicators to measure trends in economic growth.

Epilogue:
The Next Ten Years

TEN YEARS AGO I wrote my first book, *Getting In on the Ground Floor*. In it, I outlined my forecast for a bull market in the 1980s. Today, my predictions read pretty much like history as stocks have staged one of their biggest bull runs of this century.

In this book, I have up to now stayed away from specific forecasts. Instead, my goal has been to show you how my stock market and economic models work. The idea is to show you how to get the same results that have made me the nation's number one market timer over the past five years.

During the next few years, however, there are a few major factors that could dramatically increase the stock market's volatility. And they make it especially critical that you closely follow the indicators discussed in this book.

The American economy is in the middle of a huge transition. That's made many Americans highly uncertain about what lies ahead for the 1990s. Will we see a replay of the "happy days" from 1955 to 1965, when low inflation and steady growth ruled supreme? Or are we destined to relive some of the horrors of the hyperinflationary seventies? Even more disturbing, could some event overtake us, pushing us into the second depression of modern history?

Based on the economic and market models I've shown in this book, now in the early 1990s we have every reason to be optimistic about the next century. That means the economy should grow at a sustainable long-term rate. The next few years, however, could get quite rocky.

The long-term positive picture gets back to the most immutable reason of all, changing demographics. America is getting older and more frugal. Less spending and more saving means less price pressure and lower inflation.

At the same time, the graying of the nation also means that the growth in the labor force is slowing. That fact promises to shake up the way America does business, increasing productivity and boosting the nation's real (inflation-adjusted) income.

During the 1970s and 1980s, the labor force grew rapidly, due in large part to the coming of age of the baby-boom generation and increased female participation in the labor force. The rapid growth gave American business a tremendous source of inexpensive labor. Consequently, companies relied more on labor and less on capital for production.

There were several drawbacks. First, growth in productivity—the amount of goods turned out per laborer—began to slow to almost zero. Since rising productivity is the major downward force on prices long-term, falling productivity meant more upward pressures on prices, hence inflation. That's one reason why inflation has remained so ill-behaved, despite the most resolute efforts to bring it down.

Thanks to technical innovation and dramatic restructuring, manufacturing productivity continued to grow at a solid rate during that period. But because the manufacturing sector has shrunk from 80 percent of the total workforce twenty years ago to only 20 percent today, its influence has declined dramatically.

In contrast, productivity in the burgeoning service sector fell to nearly zero in the past twenty years. That's far outweighed gains in manufacturing and it's why today's productivity problem is primarily a service-sector problem. When you talk about overall economic health, you are really talking about the health of the service sector of our economy.

The second problem brought about by rapid labor force growth is a large and growing disparity in income between rich and poor. The major reason for this is that a rising pool of workers in a labor-intensive industry tends to tilt the balance of power in labor-management relations toward the managers. The number of workers per manager and per business owner, for example, has grown by leaps and bounds over the past twenty years. Another factor is the Reagan-led tax breaks for the wealthy, which spurred a significant redistribution of income from poor and middle class Americans to the wealthy.

These changes, of course, have been touted by many on Wall Street as positive for long-run economic growth. Giving the wealthy more money, it is argued, increases investment, which in turn fires up the whole economy.

The evidence, however, gives a resounding thumbs down to this approach. In fact, a relatively equitable distribution of income, rising worker productivity, and growth in real incomes are part of overall good economic health. The postwar years 1947–69 were the most recent golden age of the U.S. economy. It was a period in which worker productivity, real incomes, and annual stock market returns were at highs. Inflation was well behaved.

It was also a period in which income equality increased. In 1947, individuals in the top 5 percent accounted for 17.2 percent of total income, while those in the bottom 20 percent accounted for only 5 percent. By 1969, the upper 5 percent's share had been reduced to 15.6 percent while the bottom 20 percent accounted for 5.6 percent.

In contrast, the past twenty years or so have been marked by growing income inequality among Americans. Since 1972, the American worker's real or inflation-adjusted earnings have been pushed into a steady decline (see chart). Falling real earnings have meant Americans

REAL WEEKLY WAGES

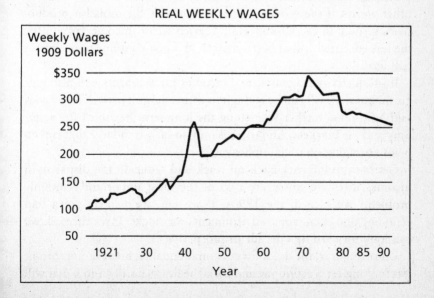

can afford to buy less, and this has crippled long-term economic growth.

Not coincidentally, productivity has fallen, U.S. companies have steadily lost markets to overseas competitors, and inflation has remained stubbornly high. Also, despite the stock market's massive upmove in the 1980s, real (inflation-adjusted) multiyear rates of return for stocks are still just breaking into positive territory. No matter how you slice it, income inequality is not good for either the economy or stocks long-term.

How serious are America's problems today? Consider the following quote: "The most pressing social challenge developed countries face . . . will be to raise the productivity of service workers. Unless this challenge is met, the developed world will face increasing social tensions, increasing polarization, increasing radicalization, possibly even class war."

If you think that quote is from a middle-aged hippie speaking off the record in a *Mother Jones* interview, think again. The speaker was Peter Drucker, arguably the most distinguished management consultant in the country. The publication was the *Harvard Business Review*.

What Drucker argued is that raising service sector productivity and reducing income disparity are really two sides of the same coin. In other words, if the economy does not provide the tools for productivity growth in the all-important service sector, income growth for the less educated will at best stagnate, at worst continue to decline in real terms.

If productivity stagnates, real incomes for managers will also languish. But that will still be enough to widen the gulf between the haves and have-nots, further worsening the long-term health of the economy and the markets. And there is only so far a trend like that can go before bringing on social upheaval.

Getting productivity back on track and reducing the disparity in incomes in this country are two of the most important economic problems we face in the 1990s. If we fail, we'll likely see a bad economy and even worse environments for stocks. If we succeed, we can look forward to a decade of prosperity.

Unfortunately, the quest for economic equality, however important it is for long-term economic and social health, is hardly a goal that will motivate businesses to seek to increase service sector productivity. Instead, the motivation will come from slowing growth in the labor force. But even motivation is not enough.

A hungry rat is motivated to find food at the end of the maze. But unless he can open the intervening doors, he is going to starve. Like the hungry rat, in other words, we Americans won't be able to satisfy our need for higher productivity, unless we have the right tools to help us.

Fortunately, we have in our hands the tools we need to make it all happen. And that's why I'm so optimistic about the decade ahead. In fact, many of you almost surely have some contact with this magnificent piece of technology nearly every day of your lives. I'm talking about the personal, or micro, computer.

Now I can hear you saying that the PC has been around for nearly twenty years. And all the while, service productivity growth has been declining, not rising. In fact, you may even wonder if the PC is the problem, not the solution.

I suggest a quick look at the history of other major technological innovations that went on to revolutionize society forever. The electric motor, for example, was available for more than twenty years before it transformed the factory workplace in the 1920s. At the turn of the century, the electric motor was a nuisance. Large and cumbersome, it was the heart of an almost unfathomable complex of shafts and pulleys that powered hundreds of different machines. The smallest glitch would shut down the entire factory. It wasn't until electric motors became small enough to power individual machines that a productivity revolution began.

Similarly, I expect the 1990s to witness the transformation of the PC from a complicated typewriter to a multiuser, multitask tool that is completely integrated with the workplace. In other words, the PC is metamorphosing from an obstacle to a high-powered facilitator of growth. Like the electric motor, it already enables one person to perform the work of 5, 10, or 100 people, in less time. And the best is yet to come.

As the 1990s progress, more advanced software and ever-finer miniaturization will make the computer a nearly ubiquitous part of our environment. Mark Weiser, the head of the redoubtable Palo Alto Research Center, envisions a world in which the computer becomes as much a part of our environment as ink. In other words, the computer will become inextricably tied to the most routine activities. Ever greater productivity gains should follow.

As these applications become more and more a part of the way America does business, service sector productivity will increase. That, combined with a shrinking labor force, should create a more equal distribution of workplace power and income. The result: The American economy should enter a new decade of prosperity, characterized by low inflation and sustainable economic growth. That's the best news possible for stocks. And it means there's a lot of money to be made in the 1990s.

The problem facing us as investors and citizens is that the transition to this rosy future will almost surely *not* be smooth and simple. For, while I do feel confident that the combination of a slowing labor force and greater use of the computer will solve our most pressing economic and social problems, many of my key long-term indicators—such as skyrocketing commodity prices—are telling me, here in mid-1994, the transition could be tumultuous.

Although I will leave long-term forecasting to another book, I can tell you now also that very high P/Es, rapid growth in M1, and a very wide spread between long- and short-term rates suggest that inflation will become more of a problem in the early to middle nineties than is now commonly thought. And if inflation is a problem, stocks are going to struggle.

Pure and simple, that is the chief lesson of this book. In order to profit fully from the transition to noninflationary growth that I envision from now on, you are going to have to pay especially close attention to all the indicators that I have outlined in the preceding pages of this book.

You'll have to be ready to move in when the indicators flash green, and get out when they flash red. And you'll have to watch your stocks carefully, to be sure you're holding strong dominant companies and avoiding the market's dogs and fallen angels.

If you follow my indicators carefully, you should have no problem meeting the challenges ahead. As I've said, all it takes is a five-dollar calculator and the time it takes to use it. That will be the difference between making money on Wall Street and losing your shirt.

Appendix:

For More Information

Barron's
This weekly publication is valuable for its "Market Week" section, a databank of market data ranging from stock trading information to economic indicators. Information can be found on the following indicators in this book: Standard and Poor's 400 price-to-earnings ratios and dividend yields, M1 and M2 money supply measures (with year-earlier levels), long- and short-term interest rates (with year-earlier levels), unemployment levels (with year-ago figures), and producer and consumer price indexes (with year-ago figures).

  Barron's can be found at most newsstands on Saturdays. To order a year's subscription, write to Dow Jones and Co., 200 Burnette Road, Chicopee, MA 01020 ($119/year).

Commerce Department Survey of Current Business
This monthly publication is by far the best resource for following the indicators in this book, and for working the market models. Both current and historical information is listed. The *Survey* can be intimidating at first, due to the large volume of statistics reported within. But fortunately, data are reported in generally the same place in every issue.

  To review the location of the indicators in this book: Bureau of Labor Statistics Industrial Commodity Price Index (page C-3, section #7 Prices, series 23), Initial State Unemployment Insurance Claims (page C-1, section #1, series 5, Average Weekly Initial Claims for Unemployment Insurance), Interest rates (page C-5, section #12 Money, Credit, Interest Rates, Stock Prices, series 114, 115, 116), Money Supply (page C-4, series 105, 106), and Corporate Net Cash Flow in billions (page C-4, section #8 Profits and Cash Flow, series 35).

To order this invaluable resource, write to Superintendent of Documents, U.S. Government Printing Office, Washington, DC 20402, or call 202-783-3238 ($34/year).

Commodity Research Bureau Commodity Index Report

This weekly report contains trading information for all commodities, including our key Bureau of Labor Statistics Industrial Price Index. It's ideal for those who want to trade commodities as well.

To order, contact the Commodity Research Bureau at 30 South Wacker Street, Suite 1820, Chicago, IL 60606, or call 800-621-5271 ($225/year).

Federal Reserve Money Stock Release

This weekly publication can't be beaten for current information on money supply measures from M1 to L. For historical information on the money supply, the Fed's Freedom of Information Department is your best source.

To order the *Money Stock Release*, contact the Fed's Publications Office at 20th and C Streets, NW, Washington, DC 20551, or call 202-452-3245. To contact the Freedom of Information Department, call 202-452-3864.

A Monetary History of the United States: 1867–1960

Written by legendary economist Milton Friedman and Anna Schwartz, this is your best resource for a very long-term history of the money supply. It's also the bible for central bankers worldwide. Its tenets have shaped economic policies for many nations for years. Found in most libraries, this book is must reading for those who want to understand the way modern economics works.

The Big Picture/Personal Finance/Utility Forecaster

If you want a service that calculates the models in this book for you, my best suggestion is to take out a subscription to one of our investment newsletters: *The Big Picture, Personal Finance*, or *Utility Forecaster*.

Of the three, *The Big Picture* ($175/12 monthly issues) is the most technical. Each issue reports on each of the indicators followed in this book. There's a portfolio for long-term investors based on my twelve-month market model and a trading portfolio based on more short-term indicators I've developed.

Like *The Big Picture*, biweekly *Personal Finance* ($118/year) also publishes the results of my market model in each issue. However, the focus is more on longer-term investing, including portfolios for conservative retirees, mutual fund investors, and long-term savers. More conservative investors may be interested in *Roger Conrad's Utility Forecaster* ($89/12 monthly issues), which covers electric, gas, water, tele-cable, and foreign utility stocks and funds.

To order any of these publications or to request a complimentary sample copy, write to KCI Communications at 1101 King Street, Suite 400, Alexandria, VA 22314, or call 800-832-2330.

The Wall Street Journal

This Monday-through-Friday paper has been America's premier business paper since 1889. I find its coverage of broad investment themes to be invaluable, and essential reading for studying the mood of the market. Most of the indicators reported in this book are also reported within its pages from time to time. However, I find the *Survey of Current Business*'s (see p. 183) presentation is much easier to use for calculating the models in this book.

The *Journal* can be found at almost any newsstand in America. To order a year's subscription, write to Dow Jones and Co., 200 Burnette Road, Chicopee, MA 01020 ($149/year).

Index

PPI pp 10   long term   source pp 15

CPI - PPI pp. 12   interim term

BLS pp. 19   this year   "   pp 183

Similar

unemployment insurance claims pp 33 (source 33 or 38 pp)

Real Interest rate: ppi - yield on 20 yr. AAA corp rate (47 p)

— Money supply
    Rule of three (3 months moving Average for 3 months) (66 p)
    Delta-m (pp 65)
    Monthly change in m2 (pp 66)